I Love the World—

It's People I Can't Stand!

Jonah's Journey of Brokenness
and Yours

ENDORSEMENTS

Insightful and profound. Simple and humorous. It will depend upon the reader which pair of adjectives seem most appropriate. Fitting to the book of Jonah, Dave takes us through the swells of the tale allowing us to experience excitement, fear, humor, and fascination that has made it [Jonah] the story of Sunday school lore with a very adult twist.

While worth reading as a stand-alone book, I longed for my small group to discuss the questions provided. Unlike many such materials, interactive dialogue genuinely appropriate to the biblical text and teaching is encouraged. Expect to go from a cartoon understanding of Jonah to an adult challenge hard to forget.

The clarity of Dave's writing style is pleasantly combined with fearlessly addressing challenging historical and intellectual queries about the text. Lest one get sidetracked by such discussions, a quick turn finds the reader challenged to consider their own life way below the surface. One can only hope this is the first of many more studies like this from this writer's quill.

—Dr. John A. Bash, Church Planter and Executive Coaching, J. Bash & Associates

Have you ever heard of this Dave Beckwith fellow? If not, let me tell you I have known him for a very long time—all the way back to boyhood days, through high school and college, during pastoral ministry and organizational leadership, now as a director of a vital restoration ministry—and I can vouch for him. He's the real deal. You will find his exposé of Jonah to be interesting, enlightening, funny, and helpful. He will show you how you can move from brokenness to wholeness.

—**Bob Thune,** Senior Pastor and Recipient of the Lifetime Achievement Award from Biola University

Dave captures the essence of seeing our own wrong responses and correcting them from God's point of view. He reminds us that when we are at our lowest, God is still at his highest and that mending brokenness comes after our surrender. It showed me how anger, disobedience, selfishness, and being judgmental have hindered my ability to love and serve as God loves and serves me.

—**Ed Fleming,** Pastor and Shepherd, Standing Stone Ministry

I have followed Jesus for 25 years. Throughout my personal faith journey, I have found myself running to God over and over. More than I'd like to admit, I've also had to stop running from God time and time again. This is why the story of Jonah resonates so deeply with me. Dave Beckwith captures the power of Jonah's story so precisely. He absolutely connects the historical-textual reality of Jonah's story with the applicable-practical crossroads of our lives today. Through this marvelous reminder of Jonah's story, Dave places the entire adventure of our running and returning firmly in God's strong and merciful hands.

—**Dr. Jeremy K. Bratcher,** Lead Pastor, Cornerstone Church and Kairos Faculty, Sioux Falls Seminary

Dr. Dave Beckwith is a seasoned soldier of the cross with many years of teaching and practical ministry under his belt. His practical insights into the life of the prophet Jonah will bless you as you reflect upon your daily spiritual journey in following Christ.

—**Frank Winans,** Senior Pastor, Woodbridge Church, Irvine, California

Although I have studied and spoken on Jonah, I gleaned so much from David Beckwith's book, *I Love the World—It's People I Can't Stand.* That certainly describes Jonah and most of us to some degree. Whether you want to work on your people loving skills or learn more about the book of Jonah and Jonah's motives, you will greatly benefit from this wonderful book. Plus, Pastor Beckwith includes thought-provoking sections which help you apply the information, share with others what you've learned or lead a small group. It's obvious David is a master writer who weaves stories, biblical insights, practical instruction, and encouragement throughout this book. I know I'll recommend this book to many. You will too.

—**Kathy Collard Miller,** International speaker and author of more than fifty books including *Pure-Hearted: The Blessings of Living Out God's Glory*

I Love the World—

It's People I Can't Stand!

Jonah's Journey of Brokenness and Yours

Dave Beckwith

PUBLISHING THE POSITIVE

ELK LAKE PUBLISHING INC
Plymouth, Massachusetts

DEDICATION

To my wife, Joanne, as we celebrate fifty years of marriage.

Traveler with me in my journey of brokenness and renewal.

A constant encourager and a friend like no other.

One in a million.

TABLE OF CONTENTS

FOREWORD

Have you ever been asked by a friend to do something so important, so honoring, that the way you do it could put your very friendship at risk? That is what I was facing when Dave Beckwith honored me with his request to write the foreword for this book.

People who have never authored a book might not realize that in many ways it is like giving birth to a child. When the book seed is placed in a person's heart and mind, it goes through an incubation period lasting several months or even longer. You can feel it growing inside. It is a struggle. It is painful. It is exciting but can produce feelings of fearful vulnerability. The final writing exposes the author to judgments, criticisms, and potential pain and heartache.

And yet, I was handed this precious "baby" by Dr. Beckwith and asked to share my thoughts with you. Would I like it? Would I consider it worth the time investment? What if I disagreed with his positions, opinions, and conclusions? I guess I could choose to make an excuse and bow out of the process altogether, but then how could I look into the eyes of a friend, a partner in ministry, someone that I highly respect and appreciate?

As I began reading, *I Love the World—It's People I Can't Stand*, I discovered a book that was clever, humorous, and insightful. The more I read, the greater the relief I experienced. I didn't just like this book, *I loved it*! I have read and preached the story of

Jonah dozens of times over decades of pastoral ministry, and yet this book helped me not just to learn more about the subject matter, but how to overcome some of the greatest obstacles we face when dealing with our raw and hard to control emotions. The same emotional conflicts Jonah experienced on his journey are the same disappointments, heartaches, anger, and feelings of depression that many of us battle on our personal journeys.

This book is worthy of your time and reflective consideration. I am convinced that most people in our churches today would highly benefit from reading it. As for me, I have been blessed, encouraged, and inspired by the words written by my friend and colleague. I enthusiastically endorse this book and encourage everyone to read it, then share it with your friends!

—**Dr. Kenneth Eichler,** Director of Ministry**,** Standing Stone Ministry

CHAPTER ZERO

EVERYONE LOVES A GREAT STORY

"Even when my teeth are gone, I'll still love a good story."

Jonah … a fascinating and intriguing story. One of the best you'll ever read. A run-away-preacher, scared-out-of-their-wits sailors, a hurricane-like storm, a fish-eats-man drama, a bleached prophet, and terrified terrorists. Further, it's true—all of it.

Jonah is not your run-of-the-mill prophet. He's different. Defiant. A rebel. Hard-headed and stubborn. Most prophets *ran to God*. Jonah *ran from God*. The prophets proclaimed their message. Jonah proclaimed his woes. Jonah's message was eight words, "'Yet forty days and Nineveh will be overthrown'" (Jonah 3:4). Lousy sermon from my perspective—no introduction, no outline, no humor, no hope, and a total downer.

Most of the prophets suffered horrific persecution. They were mocked, stoned, imprisoned, and beaten. Not Jonah. His only suffering was self-inflicted. Most of the prophets predicted the future with glimpses of hope. Jonah fumed about the future—angry there was hope. Jonah was the only prophet sent to preach in a foreign land … and the only one to run the opposite direction to a different foreign land. Jonah had more visible results than all the other prophets combined—and he deserved his success the least. God's patience with Jonah stretches the meaning of the word.

The glowing grandeur of the book is God's compassion for the undeserving—Jonah, the sailors, the terrorists in Nineveh. Above all the miracles and spectacular twists of events, nothing is of greater significance than God's love for a wicked-to-the-core people. The message of the book crashes through all the barriers of nationalism and racial hatred. People of other cultures, languages, and colors of skin matter to God. The message of the book captures the *why* for going to the ends of the earth with the good news that God loves and is willing to save the most lost person on the planet.

Perhaps, there's never been a time when the message of this book has been more needed. Racism, prejudice, and hatred flourish in our world. Many pat themselves on the back for being a loving person while they despise the person who mows their lawn … or their co-worker … or the person in the other political party … or obnoxious Uncle Charlie. Saying you love all the people in Africa and Asia is fairly easy but quite a different matter when they move into the neighborhood. God's love through Jesus Christ is for every person—murderer, kidnapper, terrorist, thief, drug addict, sexual deviant, and the self-righteous. The "Go and preach" of the opening verse of Jonah is still the command today. You cannot say the word "gospel" without saying "go."

As you capture the passion of God for a lost people and his love for a hurting world today, translate the lessons of the book into your world. Love that person who irritates you or misuses you or maligns you. Walk across the room to talk to that person others avoid. Show and tell others how much God loves them. The message of Jonah is for today!

—Pastor Dave Beckwith

I always appreciate a road map of the journey, so I created this snapshot of the contents of the book of Jonah.

The Compassion of God for the Lost			
"Should I not have compassion on Nineveh, the great city?" (4:11 NASB).			
Jonah Runs from God	Jonah Swallowed by the Fish	Jonah Preaching in Nineveh	Jonah Angry with God
Stubborness	Surrender	Serving	Self-pity
Running	Praying	Preaching	Complaining
In a ship	In a fish	In the city	In the sun
Chapter 1	Chapter 2	Chapter 3	Chapter 4
The people of Nineveh believed God's message, and from the greatest to the least, they declared a fast (3:5 NLT).			
Jonah			
Time Period: 782-753 B.C.			Writer: Jonah

CHAPTER ONE

BREAKING THE GRIP OF FEAR

A father was concerned for his son who was planning to study for a doctorate degree in Europe. The school was well known for its attacks on the Bible and Christianity. Before leaving, the father cautioned him, "Son, they will take the Book away from you. When you get back, you will no longer believe Jonah is in the Book."

His son went overseas, completed the course of study, and when he returned, his father said, "Son, is Jonah still in the Book?"

The son replied, "Dad, you find me Jonah in the Bible."

His father got out his Bible and began to flip through the pages looking for the book of Jonah. "Let's see," he mumbled, "Jonah … small book in the Minor Prophets … it's in here I know." After several minutes of searching, he still couldn't find Jonah.

With a grin, the son replied, "Dad, when I left home three years ago, I cut the book of Jonah out of your Bible, and you haven't even missed it."[1]

---

1. Harold Lindsell, "Reflections," *Decision*, May 1981, 13.

While most are familiar with the story of Jonah, this great book could be clipped from many Bibles without being missed for years. Tucked away in the Minor Prophets, Jonah is minor in length but not content. Some of the "dynamite" truths of the Bible are in the Minor Prophets.

Jonah, as we'll discover, was running from God ... and probably running for his life as well. Ninevites were terrorists. The terrorism of Islamic radicals today is nothing new. The mass killings of Hitler, Stalin, and Pol Pot of Cambodia differed only in methodology and numbers. Routinely, the Assyrians mutilated any who opposed them—cutting off hands, ears, putting out eyes or incinerating them in big heaps. Even children were burned alive at the stake. This prompted such dread and fear that entire towns would commit mass suicide rather than fall into the hands of the brutal Assyrians. Jonah must have wondered, *Preach to these savages? You've got to be out of your mind.* There is no excusing his defiance of God, but when we get a picture of the horrific deeds of the Ninevites, we begin to understand Jonah's fears.

Who are the terrorists in your life? Not the "strapping bombs to their bodies or threatening to kill or imprison you" terrorists. Cantankerous and malicious people who strike terror in your heart. You feel dread and fear every time you think about them. Your anxiety may be an unreasonable, demanding boss, or a neighbor you'd be glad never to see again. Or someone who hurt you deeply and never acknowledged their wrong.

The "I Love the World—It's People I Can't Stand!" is a disconnect of intentionality and behavior. The two phrases don't belong together. They are incongruent. Most of us think of ourselves as a loving person, but truth be told, there are some people we can't stand—and we're not about to go out of our way to be loving to them. At the root of this is fear, we fear what they may do to us or demand of us. We may also fear them for what they have done to us. They may be perceived as bullies, abrasive, or obnoxious. Or they may be crazy-makers—charming and powerful personalities who are very destructive. They are "unsafe people." This chapter is about "breaking the grip of fear" which kinks our love cord—our capacity to love the unlovable.

But first, let's discuss whether Jonah was a mythological person in a fanciful tale, or whether Jonah was a real person in an accurate historical account.

WAS JONAH "FOR REAL"?

The word of the LORD came to Jonah son of Amittai ...
(Jonah 1:1)

Many critics have attempted to peg Jonah as a fictional character in a mythical allegory ... sort of an ancient Wizard of Oz story. Why? Skeptics who have difficulty swallowing the miracles in Jonah (particularly Jonah living three days in a fish), conveniently label the story as an allegory. For example, one allegorical approach places the writing of Jonah in 430 BC instead of 760 BC. "In this view, Jonah represents disobedient Israel; the sea represents the Gentiles; the great fish, Babylon; and the three days in the fish's belly, the Babylonian captivity of the Jews."[2] Far-fetched, fanciful imagination becomes the norm for interpretation.

---

2. Charles Ryrie, *Ryrie Study Bible* (Chicago: Moody Press, 1978), 1376.

The Facts

Are the details in the book accurate and reliable? Was Jonah for real? Here are the historical facts.

Fact 1: Jonah was a real person, and his father is identified. Jonah, whose name in Hebrew means "dove," is introduced as the son of Amittai in Jonah 1:1. Real people have real fathers.

Fact 2: Jonah's home town is named and geographically identified. According to 2 Kings 14:23–25, Jonah came from a town called Gath-hepher, located three miles northeast of Jesus' hometown of Nazareth.[3] Real people come from real places.

Fact 3: Jonah was a recognized prophet in Israel. Identified in the national historical record, Jonah served as an accredited prophet of God to Israel. He served during the reign of King Jeroboam II (793–753 BC) in the Northern Kingdom of Israel (2 Kings 14:23–27). Thus, the events and writing of Jonah can be dated around 760 BC.

Fact 4: Jonah is mentioned by name in an important archaeological find. Discovered between 1974 and 1976, the 16,500 Ebla tablets and fragments from present-day Syria mention Jonah along with other familiar biblical names and places: Adam, Eve, Abraham, David, Ur, Sodom and Gomorrah, and Zoar.[4] Of course, names may in some cases refer to another

---

3. Irving L. Jensen, *Minor Prophets of Israel* (Chicago: Moody Press, 1975), 18.

4. Richard Ostling, "New Grounding for the Bible?" *Time*, September 21, 1981.

person or place, but the amount of biblical information and confirmation in the Ebla tablets is astounding.

Fact 5: Jesus spoke of Jonah and the events in Jonah as real and factual. Jesus gives a clear statement validating Jonah as a person three times.

> "An evil and adulterous generation craves for a sign; and yet no sign shall be given to it but the sign of Jonah the prophet; for just as JONAH WAS THREE DAYS AND THREE NIGHTS IN THE BELLY OF THE SEA MONSTER, so shall the Son of Man be three days and three nights in the heart of the earth." (Matt. 12:39–40)

> "An evil and adulterous generation seeks after a sign; and a sign will not be given it, except the sign of Jonah." (Matt. 16:4)

> "This generation is a wicked generation; it seeks for a sign, and yet no sign will be given to it but the sign of Jonah. For just as Jonah became a sign to the Ninevites, so will the Son of Man be to this generation. The Queen of the South will rise up with the men of this generation at the judgment and condemn them because she came from the ends of the earth to hear the wisdom of Solomon; and behold, something greater than Solomon is here. The men of Nineveh will stand up with this generation at the judgment and condemn it, because they repented at the preaching of Jonah; and behold, something greater than Jonah is here." (Luke 11:29–32)

What difference does it make if Jonah was a historical figure or a mythical character of folklore? The answer is simple: *If Jonah is a fictional character as some maintain, then Jesus did not speak the truth.* Many, including those who doubt Jonah was real, will quickly say Jesus Christ was a great teacher. How strange, since one of the marks of a great teacher is that what they teach is accurate and truthful. If Jesus is a great teacher, his authentication of the book of Jonah must stand.[5]

Fact 6: The character of Jonah is not mythical, but vividly real, showing his character flaws. Jonah was openly rebellious, fearful, spiritually calloused, prejudiced, paranoid, bigoted, selfish, stubborn, depressed, resistant to God's will, and suicidal. Most prophets took delight in God's will. Jonah took flight from God's will. Saint of the year? No! Real and human? Yes!

Fact 7: The traditional burial place for Jonah is in the ancient city of Nineveh, the current city of Mosul, Iraq. On July 24, 2014, ISIS militants took sledgehammers to the tomb of the prophet Jonah and planted explosives around the site and blew it up. Perhaps Jonah repented and returned to Nineveh to minister to the people he detested and was finally buried there.

According to Jewish Tradition, Jonah was the man brought back to life by God through the prophet Elisha. I don't include this as a fact since it is a rabbinic tradition, but the legend raises an interesting possibility. This is what we know to be true. A well-to-do woman living in Shunem extended hospitality to the prophet Elisha. She prepared a room for him with a bed, table,

---

5. J. Vernon McGee, *Thru the Bible: Proverbs Through Malachi* (Nashville: Thomas Nelson Publishers, 1982), 738.

chair, and lamp—a prophet's chamber. Advanced in age, she was grieving that she did not have a son. Elisha learned of her yearning to have a son and told her, "'Next year at this time you will be holding a son in your arms!' 'No, my lord!' she cried. 'O man of God, don't deceive me and get my hopes up like that'" (2 Kings 4:16 NLT).

Despite her husband's and her advanced ages, she became pregnant and gave birth to a son just as Elisha had told her. The child grew and one day developed a severe headache (2 Kings 4:19). She held him on her lap until noon, and then he died.

In bitter distress, she sought out Elisha who returned with her to the bedside of her dead son.

> When Elisha came into the house, behold the lad was dead and laid on his bed. So he entered and shut the door behind them both and prayed to the LORD. And he went up and lay on the child, and put his mouth on his mouth and his eyes on his eyes and his hands on his hands, and he stretched himself on him; and the flesh of the child became warm. Then he returned and walked in the house once back and forth, and went up and stretched himself on him; and the lad sneezed seven times and the lad opened his eyes. He called Gehazi and said, "Call this Shunammite." So he called her. And when she came in to him, he said, "Take up your son." Then she went in and fell at his feet and bowed herself to the ground, and she took up her son and went out. (2 Kings 4:32–37)

All this is fact. Here's the Jewish tradition: *the boy raised to life was Jonah!*[6] Further, some scholars believe Jonah was a student of Elisha.

---

6. W.H. Winkler, *The Book of Jonah* (Bloomington, IN: Westbow Press, 2018), 32.

Without a doubt, Jonah was for real—a defiant, stubborn prophet who dared to disobey God.

WHY DID JONAH RUN?

Jonah rose up to flee to Tarshish from the presence of the Lord. (Jonah 1:3)

The stunning disobedience of Jonah sets the drama for all that takes place in the book and displays the mercy of God in giving him a second calling, a second opportunity. Why did Jonah do something so foolish? What was driving his disobedience? I believe Jonah was driven by two things: prejudice and paranoia.

PREJUDICE

Arise, go to Nineveh the great city and cry against it, for their wickedness has come up before Me. (Jonah 1:2)

Billy Graham took a courageous stand against racial prejudice during his Crusade in Chattanooga, Tennessee, in 1953. At the time, common practice called for ropes to separate the whites seated in the front and blacks in the back. When Billy walked into the crusade, he saw the ropes and was appalled by it. He went to the head usher and asked him to remove the ropes. He refused, so Billy took the ropes down himself. The head usher resigned in a huff creating quite a stir, but Graham's stand led the way for breaking down walls of prejudice.[7]

God hates racial prejudice. The imaginary story of a black man who was attempting to join a snobbish white church makes the point. Every time the black man sought to become part of

7. "Taking Down the Ropes—Part 2," *YouTube*, Billy Graham Evangelistic Association, published Jan. 8, 2018, accessed Mar. 31, 2019, https://www.youtube.com/watch?v=EQuFvvwnKRE.

the congregation, the prejudiced congregation turned him away. Distressed, he went to the Lord in prayer pleading as to why he had been rejected time and time again. The Lord offered comfort and understanding and added, "Don't worry, my son. I've been trying to get in that church myself for forty years."[8]

Jonah, like the cartoon character Charlie Brown, likely would have said, "I love mankind—it's Ninevites I can't stand." I think Jonah would rather spit at a Ninevite than shake his hand. The thought of visiting this city, buying food, sleeping there, and associating with Ninevites must have been highly repulsive. Jonah was a bigot.

WHY DID JONAH HATE NINEVITES?

Partly because the Assyrians were the dreaded enemies of Israel, but also because the city of Nineveh was one of the "armpits of the world" morally. Speaking of Nineveh, God said, "their wickedness has come up before Me" (v. 2). Implied is a stench of immorality that would rival Sodom and Gomorrah on the all-time filth list—drunkenness, prostitution, astrology, witchcraft, extreme violence and torture, corruption, ruthless greed. Nahum 3:4 describes ancient Nineveh as the "harlotries of the harlot" and the "mistress of sorceries."

WHY WAS NINEVEH CALLED A GREAT CITY?

Not only was Nineveh a "gross city" morally, but it was also a "great city"—a designation noted four times in the book of Jonah (1:2; 3:2; 3:3; 4:11).[9] Jonah 3:3 adds a superlative calling it an

---

8. Herb Walker, *The Happy Clergy* (Amarillo, TX: Baxter Lane Co., 1977), 27.

9. The word "great" is used several times in Jonah: Nineveh the great city (1:2; 3:2; 3:3; 4:11), the great wind and storm (1:4, 12), the great fish (1:17), and the great deep of the ocean (2:5 NASB). God shows himself to be greater than all the greatness revealed in the book.

"exceedingly great city." Located on the Tigris River, historians and archaeologists confirm the biblical record of Nineveh as one of the great cities of the ancient world. *The International Standard Bible Encyclopedia (ISBE)* says the defensive wall of the city likely measured fifty feet thick (wide enough for more than four lanes of freeway traffic—eleven feet per lane) and a hundred feet high (one-third the length of a football field on end).[10] One of the greatest ancient libraries has been discovered in the ruins of Nineveh. The Assyrians were great inventors, inventing paved roads, locks and keys, the first postal system, plumbing and flush toilets, a method of keeping time, and ways of using iron.[11] They also initiated the practice of astrology and were the first to give names to the signs of the Zodiac.[12]

The recent archaeological discovery of the tablets of Ebla, one of the most remarkable archaeological finds ever, demonstrates the advancement of the Ninevites in astronomy, law, science, commerce, history, philology, literature, and religion. As mentioned earlier, the Ebla tablets mention Jonah.[13]

WHAT IS THE FIRST MENTION OF NINEVEH IN THE BIBLE?

Nimrod, a son of Cush and a great warrior and hunter, established Babylon as well as Nineveh (Gen. 10:8–12). He went on to build the Tower of Babel. Nineveh became the "great city"—the greatest in the world at that time. As a result of Jonah's preaching, the city of Nineveh repented of their sin, and God withheld judgment.

10. *The International Standard Bible Encyclopedia (ISBE)*, 4th ed. (1955) s.v. "Nineveh."
11. Winkler, *Jonah* 26.
12. *ISBE,* s.v. "Library of Nineveh."
13. Ostling, "New Grounding," *Time,* 76–77.

WHAT BECAME OF NINEVEH?

The Ninevites relapsed. About a hundred years after Jonah, the prophet Nahum (writing in about 661 BC) predicted the destruction and fall of Nineveh. He prophesied that the city, in a state of drunkenness (Nah. 1:10), would be destroyed in an overflowing flood (1:8; 2:6) and burned (3:13). While under siege, history records the Ninevites felt secure in their mighty city with large amounts of food stored away. After three years and heavy rains, the river swelled and broke down part of the city walls just as Nahum had prophesied fifty years earlier. Nineveh was laid waste by the armies of the Babylonians, the Medes, and Scythians about 612 BC. Nahum further prophesied the destruction would be like an incurable wound, the injury would be fatal, and the city would become desolate (3:19). The troops of Alexander the Great, three hundred years later, couldn't even find a trace of the city. Today the ruins are opposite the city of Mosul, and the city has been completely excavated.

HOW LARGE WAS THE GREAT CITY OF NINEVEH?

Historical evidence indicates Nineveh (including the surrounding district) was the largest city in the world at that time. Population for the district has been estimated to be about one million. The basis for this estimate is discussed later.

Preaching to this enormous city could be intimidating, but more paralyzing was Jonah's fierce hatred of the city's inhabitants. They wanted to destroy Israel. Today, this would be like a Jew from Israel being called of God to preach judgment in downtown Tehran, Iran, the country that wants to wipe them off the face of the earth. To Jonah, the assignment must have seemed bizarre. He also knew if they repented, God would forgive them. Later in the story, we see Jonah "red hot" angry when God forgave them rather than destroying them (Jonah 4:1). In his religious and racial bigotry, Jonah looked down his self-righteous nose at the despicable citizens of Nineveh, hoping they would be destroyed.

PARANOIA

> Jonah rose up to flee to Tarshish from the presence of the LORD. So he went down to Joppa, found a ship which was going to Tarshish, paid the fare and went down into it to go with them to Tarshish from the presence of the LORD. (Jonah 1:3)

Behind Jonah's bigotry was the close cousin of prejudice, *fear*! And Jonah had good reason to fear the Ninevites.

Famed for their advanced civilization, the Assyrians were even more famous for their methods of torture and conquest by cruelty. Nahum the prophet gives a gripping description of Nineveh.

> What sorrow awaits Nineveh, the city of murder and lies! She is crammed with wealth and is never without victims. Hear the crack of whips, the rumble of wheels! Horses' hooves pound, and chariots clatter wildly. See the flashing swords and glittering spears as the charioteers charge past! There are countless casualties, heaps of bodies—so many bodies that people stumble over them. All this because Nineveh, the beautiful and faithless city, mistress of deadly charms, enticed the nations with her beauty. She taught them all her magic, enchanting people everywhere. (Nah. 3:1–4 NLT)

The greatness of the Assyrians was achieved via their brutality. For example:

> They used very cruel methods of torture and could extract information from their captives very easily. One of the procedures was to take a man out onto the sands of the desert and bury him up to his neck—nothing

but his head would stick out. Then they would put a thong through his tongue and leave him there to die as the hot, penetrating sun would beat down upon his head. It is said that a man would go mad before he died. That was one of the "nice little things" the Assyrians hatched up.[14]

On one of the tablets which archaeologists have found, Esarhaddon (687–642 BC), the Assyrian Monarch, is shown holding "two captive princes on strings tied to hooks through their lips."[15] The Assyrian army traveled with their families. The scene of this mob moving across the land struck total panic in their enemies, "… when they moved down like a plague of locusts upon a town or village, it is said that they were so feared and dreaded that on some occasions an entire town would commit suicide rather than fall into the hands of the brutal Assyrians."[16]

An earlier ruler, Ashur-nasirpal II (883–859 BC) had a reputation for cruelty that probably made Jonah's toes curl.

> His usual procedure after the capture of a hostile city was to burn it, and then to mutilate all the grown male prisoners by cutting off their hands and ears and putting out their eyes; after which they were piled up in a great heap to perish in torture from sun, flies, their wounds and suffocation; the children, both boys and girls, were all burnt alive at the stake; and the chief was carried off to Assyria to be flayed alive for the king's delectation.[17]

One of the monuments discovered in Nineveh states, "Many within the border of my own land, I flayed and spread their

---

14. McGee, *Thru the Bible*, 742.

15. Edward M. Blaiklock and R. K. Harrison, eds., *The New International Dictionary of Biblical Archaeology* (Grand Rapids: Zondervan Publishing House, 1983), p. 339.

16. McGee, *Thru the Bible*, 742.

17. H.R. Hall, *The Ancient History of the Near East*, p445, quoted in Irving L. Jensen, *Minor Prophets of Israel* (Chicago: Moody Press, 1975), 26–27.

skins upon the walls."[18] These people were skinned alive, and their skins hung on the city walls.

Jonah must have thought, *Ninevites would love to cut off my hands, put out my eyes, skin me alive, and hang my hide on a wall ... and you want me to preach to these terrorists. And what if they repent? You'll just forgive them as if they've done nothing wrong? Absurd. Unthinkable. I'm getting as far from Nineveh as I can.*

WHY DO WE RUN?

Jonah is running from his God assignment. We've probably all had a time when we wanted to run the other direction. Our life may not be physically threatened, but none-the-less we feel threatened. We run for several reasons.

First, we may *run* because we want to *run* our own lives.

It may be a wrong relationship, a self-centered life pursuit, a self-destructive life habit. When we run from God, things get tangled in a hurry—relationships go sour, frustration replaces fulfillment, and our future begins to look gloomy and stormy. Trouble's ahead, but we charge forward.

Second, we may run because we have been hurt or wounded by someone.

Rather than confront the situation, we maneuver ways to avoid the person or the situation. When I was a newspaper boy in fourth grade, I was bitten by a bulldog at one of the homes on my delivery route. I dreaded delivering the paper to that house. I'd look around the corner to see if the bulldog was outside or

---

18. David Guzik, "Nahum 3—Nineveh, The Wicked City," *Enduring Word Bible Commentary*, accessed March 31, 2019, https://enduringword.com/bible-commentary/nahum-3/.

inside the house. If the dog was inside, I would scamper to the door and leave the paper as fast I could. I didn't have the courage to tell the homeowner that I had been bitten by their dog. The bulldog won. I was miserable. I loved dogs then and still do. But at that time, I could have honestly said, "I love dogs—it's bulldogs I can't stand." How easy it is to think we're a genuine "lover of people" … except when we meet a meet a "human bulldog" we can't stand.

Third, we may run because of an unresolved conflict we don't want to face.

A conflict simmers with a boss, neighbor, church, or family member. Some may quit a good job due to an unresolved conflict—or move to another neighborhood, change churches, or leave a marriage. The bulldog wins. If you flee because of unresolved conflict, don't be surprised when you meet a similar conflict in your new situation.

I recall a family telling me they were leaving the church. When I asked why, they said, "We love the church and your teaching, but we just can't stand running into this other couple." There are times to change churches—when our spiritual growth is stagnated, our children are not fitting in, etc. However, there is a simple principle: *when we flee an unpleasant situation that God wants to use to shape us and polish our character, we will meet a similar situation in the place we flee to.* Why? God is committed to refining this area in our lives.

Fourth, like Jonah, we may run from a God assignment.

God may want you to lead or host a Bible study or Sunday school class, help the homeless, lead a ministry, witness to your neighbor. Indifference or laziness settles in, and we run by avoiding what God has for us to do.

BREAKING THE GRIP OF FEAR

"What happens if you get scared half to death twice?" baseball player Steven Wright humorously asked. Jonah was scared half to death twice—once fearing the terrorism of the Ninevites and again fearing death by drowning in the sea. Jonah was trapped, imprisoned by his fears. Our fears can be a prison. Irrational paranoia paralyzes. How do I break the strangling grip of fear or paranoia in my life?

First, identify the fears or worries that divide your mind.

The usual Greek word for "worry" (*merimnáō*) means to "divide the mind." Worry divides the thoughts, feelings, perceptions, and judgments. We are at war within ourselves. When worried, we're prone to make wrong decisions or delay making the right decision. We may become paralyzed in our thinking.

The word *fear* in the New Testament is a different word. The Greek language uses the word *phobos* from which we get the word "phobia." Fears can turn into phobias—life patterns that protect us but may also overly control us. A phobia is generally a highly focused fear of something—spiders, germs, getting cancer, intimacy, snakes, flying, etc. A rational cause for the fear can usually be found beneath a phobia—like not wanting to be bitten by a snake—but phobias can become unhealthy and interfere with normal living. For example, if you have *arithmophobia*, the fear of numbers or *somniphobia*, the fear of sleep, these fears will impair your ability to function normally. Or there is *phophobia*, the fear of fear. Believe it or not, some people have a fear of heaven called *uranophobia*. Now that is strange.

Paranoia is quite different than phobias. Paranoia is an extreme and unreasonable feeling that other people do not like you or are going to harm you. Severe paranoia may cause a person to become convinced someone is following them, intending to hurt or kill them (when no one is there). A person I saw for counseling was convinced helicopters were overhead tracking her every move. There were no helicopters, and nothing I said could convince her otherwise. These irrational thoughts may become so fixed no amount of evidence can convince them otherwise. They are driven by overwhelming, compelling emotions to do things that make no sense.

In my opinion, Jonah's disobedience in fleeing from God was completely irrational—a paranoid reaction to overwhelming fear, totally forgetting the power of God. Why would he leave his homeland for a place that was thousands of miles away? If Jonah had family or friends (and we don't know that he did), they might have tried hopelessly to talk him out of his senseless trip. Did he know anyone in Spain? Did he have a future in Spain? It's unlikely. Why didn't he just stay home and refuse to go to Nineveh? Why would a prophet of God think he could hole away in a ship and hide from God? As far as I can tell, there was not one rational reason to flee to Spain. His decision was senseless on every count. Jonah 1:3 says Jonah "paid the fare." In the Hebrew language, the word *fare* is literally "her fare." "Rabbis interpreted this to mean that Jonah bought the ship."[19] If so, Jonah's actions were whacko—total paranoia.

Second, don't fear people.

When we fear someone, we generally avoid being around them. If we're forced into contact with them, we may become

---

19. Frank E. Gaebelein, editor, *The Expositor's Bible Commentary: Daniel, Minor Prophets*, Vol. 7 (Grand Rapids, MI: Zondervan Publishing House, 1985), 370.

edgy, extremely uncomfortable, and seek ways to escape the situation. The greater the level of fear, the more we can't stand them … or stand to be around them.

Jonah obviously couldn't stand the thought of being around Ninevites. This is where he got into trouble—fearing people but not fearing God. The fear of man is a snare. It takes remarkable courage to trust God when your life is threatened.

What emotions gripped you when you viewed the media clip of Christians being murdered by Islamic extremists on a beach in Libya? Dressed in orange jumpsuits, their hands cuffed behind them, twenty-one Christians were pushed to the ground and beheaded.

On Palm Sunday of 2017, Islamic extremists blew up two churches in Egypt killing forty-five worshipers. A week later, the *Christianity Today* headline stated, "Forgiveness: Muslims Moved as Coptic Christians Do the Unimaginable." One of the widows, with her children by her side, astounded everyone when she said, "I'm not angry at the one who did this. I'm telling him, 'May God forgive you, and we also forgive you. Believe me, we forgive you.'"[20]

Amr Adeeb, perhaps the most prominent talk show host in Egypt, struggled for words to describe his emotions. For twelve seconds, there was an awkward silence which is like an eternity on television. Finally, collecting himself, he said, "How great is this forgiveness you have!" his voice cracked. "The Copts of Egypt … are made of … steel!" he finally uttered. Millions across the airwaves of Egypt marveled with him.

---

20. Jason Casper, "Forgiveness: Muslims Moved as Coptic Christians Do the Unimaginable," *Christianity Today*, April 20, 2017, accessed Mar. 31, 2019, www.christianitytoday.com/news/2017/april/forgiveness-muslims-moved-coptic-christians-egypt-isis.html

If God asked you to go to the modern city of Mosul (ancient Nineveh) or another battlefront to proclaim the gospel to Islamic extremists, how would you react? Wow! That is a scary thought.

I ask myself, *Would I be willing to go into the headquarters of murderous extremists to proclaim the gospel?* If the Lord told me to go, after recovering from the shock, I would probably ask him to clarify his instructions: *You want me to do WHAT? Are you sure about the location? Did you say Mosul or Maui?* I would be looking for signs and wet fleece and prepaid airline tickets deposited in my mailbox anonymously ... anything to make sure God was giving me the orders.

Joanne and I both prayed about going overseas to live and minister, but God made clear this was not his will for us at this time in our lives. Instead, we realized God was sending the nations to us. So, we opened our home to Muslims. Our first guest was from Saudi Arabia, and his dad was a top advisor to the King of Saudi. His sister was married into the Saud family. His family was regarded as the number two family in the kingdom. We developed a deep friendship with him which allowed us to share the gospel numerous times.

On an occasion with another Muslim guest, Joanne entered his bedroom one morning to clean. She jumped back startled and started to tremble when she saw a crescent-shaped sword on top of his prayer mat. Who had we allowed into our home? She envisioned a sword-wielding attack some night when we were asleep. Finally, she calmed her fears long enough to reach down and touch the sword. It was a plastic toy. There have been moments when we've wondered if we did the right thing, but in every case, God has provided the opportunity for long discussions about Christianity and Islam. We see a hunger for truth. Our last student asked, "Would you show me the verses in the Bible where Jesus claims to be God?" I am currently dialoguing by email with him, a brilliant Muslim studying to be a lawyer at the University of Southern California. His first question: "Let's discuss the rational evidences that prove Jesus is God, and he is the Son of God. How would you convince me of this opinion if I were an atheist?"

To pose the question again, "Who are the terrorists in your life?" Not the "strapping bombs to their bodies or threatening to kill or imprison you" terrorists. Cantankerous, malicious, or vindictive people who strike terror in your heart. You feel dread and fear every time you think about them. It may be an unreasonable, demanding boss or a neighbor who you'd be glad never to see again. Or someone who hurt you deeply and has never acknowledged their wrong. It may be your spouse or your parents. Have you ever had someone in your life so despicable and wicked that you secretly wanted them to suffer in hell? Or maybe you were open about how you felt and told them, "Go to hell … you …"? Do you realize what you just said? Don't overlook the fact that you deserve hell except for the mercy and pardon God has granted you. God doesn't want anyone to go to hell. The Lord "… is patient toward you, not wishing for any to perish but for all to come to repentance" (2 Pet. 3:9).

How do I change my attitude about people I can't stand—people who hate me, malign me, terrorize me, and make my life miserable?

Don't pull a Jonah. If you fear or despise someone, the natural tendency is to run from them or avoid them. God may want you to love them with the love that God has for you. "Therefore, accept one another, just as Christ also accepted us to the glory of God" (Rom. 15:7).

Be like Jesus. Let Jesus respond through you as he did after being falsely arrested, beaten, mocked, and hung on the cross,

"Father, forgive them; for they do not know what they are doing" (Luke 23:34).

Be like Stephen. With the ugly angry crowd stoning him to death, he cried out, "Lord, do not hold this sin against them" (Acts 7:60).

Be like Joseph. With his brothers who nearly ruined his life, he said, "You meant evil against me, but God meant it for good" (Gen. 50:20).

Third, face the future with faith instead of fear.

Fears always demand surrender. Fears are bullies. They prance around in our minds insisting we bow down to them. We either surrender to our fears, or we surrender to God in faith. Surrender to God is the key to dealing with fears. Both Jeremiah and David faced death and chose to trust God to bring them through.

Jeremiah was hated and despised. His enemies lowered him into a pit that had no water—only gooey mud. In the same way, Jeremiah sank into the mud (Jer. 38:6), it would be normal to sink in despair as well. Instead, he called on the Lord. Here's what he experienced: "Yes, you came when I called; you told me, 'Do not fear.'" (Lam. 3:57 NLT). Jeremiah surrendered to God instead of yielding to his natural fears.

David was captured by the Philistines. Obviously, they would have been eager to slay the man who killed their national hero and champion, Goliath. David worked through his fears in Psalm 56. "When I am afraid, I will put my trust in you. I praise God for what he has promised. I trust in God, so why should I be afraid? What can mere mortals do to me? … I trust in God, so why should I be afraid? What can mere mortals do to me?" (Ps. 56:3-4, 11 NLT).

Regardless of what has happened in your life—financial ruin, loss of health, family tragedy, a threat on your life, a broken relationship—God says, "Do not fear." Turn to him in faith and claim these words as your own: "I trust in God, so why should I be afraid? What can mere mortals do to me? (v. 11 NLT).

J. C. Penney was the founder of the J. C. Penney company in the early 1900s. His story is a great American success story.

But few realize that worry nearly destroyed J. C. Penney.

After the 1929 stock crash, J. C., which stood for James Cash, lost all his cash. His personal wealth was gone, and he nearly lost his life as well. For the company to survive, he borrowed against his life insurance to pay his employees. The financial losses took a toll on his mental, emotional, and physical health. The fears of what might happen consumed his mind, paralyzing his ability to work and preventing him from sleeping at night. He developed shingles, a condition that causes severe pain. He finally checked himself in at the Battle Creek Sanitarium. He was given sedatives to calm him, but they provided no relief. The combination of financial losses and worry broke him physically, emotionally, and mentally, and he was certain he would die before morning. He wrote farewell letters to his wife and son.

When he awoke the next morning, he heard singing in the hospital chapel. He made his way to the chapel and entered as the group was singing, "God Will Take Care of You." The words and music melted his fearful heart, bringing hope to his broken mind and spirit. During the Scripture reading and prayer, he surrendered his life to the care of God and was born-again.[21] J. C. Penney, in his own words, described what happened that day.

> Suddenly something happened. I can't explain it. I can only call it a miracle. I felt as if I had been instantly lifted out of the darkness of a dungeon into warm, brilliant sunlight. I felt as if I had been transported from hell to paradise. I felt the power of God as I had never felt it before. I realized then that I alone was responsible for all my troubles. I know that God with his love was there to help me.[22]

Penney's health returned, God took care of him and the chain of stores bearing his name multiplied across the country. God used him as a great philanthropist until his passing at age ninety-five.

It's a promise … *God will take care of you!*

21. *Wikipedia Encyclopedia,* s.v. "James Cash Penney," accessed March 31, 2019, wikipedia.org/wiki/James_Cash_Penney.

22. S. I. McMillen, *None of These Diseases* (Old Tappan, NJ: Fleming H. Revell Co., 1967), 96.

TIME OUT

CHAPTER ONE

BREAKING THE GRIP OF FEAR

In the pressure cooker of life, everyone needs a time out—an opportunity to recharge the emotional and spiritual batteries. The Time Outs with each chapter are designed to refresh you and deepen your walk with God.

You will notice the fish symbol with each Time Out—a simple reminder of this amazing fish story. But the fish sign has a deeper meaning.

WHAT IS THE MEANING OF THE FISH SYMBOL?

You have probably seen the fish symbol (sometimes with the Greek word *ichthus* on the inside) displayed on Bible covers, bumper stickers, or business cards, but what does it mean?

The fish symbol goes back to the early centuries of Christianity when Christians were tortured, beaten, or beheaded for their faith. Sometimes they were dipped in pitch and lit on fire while alive or torn apart by wild animals. Being a Christian was dangerous, and they needed a way to safely identify each other while affirming their faith. Since the Romans, Greeks, and other groups used the fish symbol before the Christians, the fish mark, unlike the cross, drew little suspicion. The fish made an ideal icon for persecuted believers for two reasons.

An affirmation of commitment. Christians used the fish figure to discern who the real Christians were and where they were meeting. The sympol appeared on trees, doorways, and even tombs to indicate secret places of worship. Displayed on the ouside of a home, it let other Christians know this was a place of safety and fellowship. If you visit the ancient catacombs in Rome (underground burial caverns where Christians hid and worshipped), you will see fish symbols etched on the walls.

According to tradition, Christians used the fish drawing to dtermine if someone was a Christian or not. When a Christian met a stranger on the road, the Christian would draw half of the fish symbol in the dirt. If the other person drew the second half of the fish, they knew this person was a believer.

An affirmation of belief. The fish symbol was a mini-doctrinal statement. The Greek word for fish, *ichthus*, was used as an acrostic:

I—*iesous* which means Jesus
CH—*christos* which means Christ
TH—*theo* which means God
U—*uios* which means Son
S—*soter* which means Savior

The word for fish, ichthus, was a statement of faith: *Jesus Christ God's Son Savior.* The fish symbol, then and now, is a reminder of biblical truth. Jesus rescued Jonah from the fish, fed the multitude with five loaves and two fish (Mk. 6:34–44), called his disciples to be fishers of men (Mt. 4:19), and enjoyed a fish fry with his disciples in his resurrected body (John 21:9–14). Let the fish symbol be a reminder to follow wholeheartedly the Champion of your faith: *Jesus Christ God's Son Savior.*

Ready to grow in your walk with God? Select a place free from distraction, relax, quiet yourself, and enjoy the presence of God. This is your Time Out—a much needed break from the frantic pace of life.

GROW AND APPLY

◊ Read these verses: Jonah 1:1–3, Matthew 12:39–40, Luke 11:29–32.

◊ You meet someone who says they believe Jonah is a mythological character and the lesson of Jonah is an allegory. What would you say to them?

_____

_____

_____

_____

_____

_____

◊ Read Psalm 56. David writes this section when the Philistines captured him (remember David killed their national hero and champion Goliath). He feels trapped and trampled on by his enemies. David has every reason to be scared half to death. His life was in the balance. Highlight or underline David's twice-repeated response: "When I am afraid, I will put my trust in you. I praise God for what he has promised. I trust in God, so why should I be afraid? What can mere mortals do to me? ... I trust in God, so why should I be afraid? What can mere mortals do to me?" (Ps. 56:3-4, 11 NLT).

◊ When have fears of people—what they might say, think, or do to you—been a struggle for you?

_____

_____

_____

_____

_____

_____

◊ In what ways are you a people pleaser?

_____

_____

_____

_____

_____

_____

◊ Who would you put on your list of "people I can't stand"? Are they an acquaintance, a relative, a member of the opposite sex, a fellow employee? Do they belong to a different racial group or a terrorist group? To what degree does fear contribute to your dislike of them?

_____

_____

_____

_____

_____

_____

◊ Describe when you have been at a surrender point with fear—either surrender to the fear or surrender to the Lord.

_____

_____

_____

_____

_____

_____

◊ What are your worries? Write them down. Do they divide your mind? Do you have difficulty making decisions because of worries?

_____

_____

_____

_____

_____

_____

◊ Now identify any fears or phobias you have. Which ones protect you and which ones interfere with normal living? Is there a phobia taking control of your life in an unhealthy manner?

_____

_____

_____

_____

_____

_____

_____

_____

PRAY

◊ Pray the words to the song that brought relief and salvation to J. C. Penney.

"GOD WILL TAKE CARE OF YOU"[23]
Civilla D. Martin

Be not dismayed whate'er betide,
God will take care of you;
Beneath his wings of love abide,
God will take care of you.
Refrain:
God will take care of you,
Through every day, o'er all the way;
He will take care of you,
God will take care of you.
All you may need he will provide,
God will take care of you;
Nothing you ask will be denied,
God will take care of you.

---

23. Civilla D. Martin, "God Will Take Care of You," 1904, public domain.

SHARE

This week be alert to people you meet who are fearful. Look for an opportunity to share an encouraging word or listen to their fears. Here are some thought-provoking questions that may ignite a discussion:

1. What goes through your mind when you hear of nuclear threat or terrorism in the news?
2. What do you do to cope with fear?
3. What do you think of this phrase, "I Love the World—It's People I Can't Stand?"

TIME TOGETHER

CHAPTER ONE

BREAKING THE GRIP OF FEAR

If you're leading a small group, teaching a Bible class, or sharing with the family, below are some opening questions. For the content of the lesson, use the Grow and Apply, Prayer, and Share sections with your Time Out.

In Appendix B in the back, you will find the Guide for Small Groups designed to assist you in forming and leading a small group.

CONNECT
(discussion questions)

1. What was your biggest fear when you were growing up? Are your fears different today?

_____

_____

2. If God called you to proclaim the gospel to militants who were murdering Christians, how would you feel? How would you answer?

_____

_____

_____

_____

_____

_____

CHAPTER TWO

THIS IS YOUR WAKE-UP CALL

Isn't there a more pleasant way to begin a day than an alarm clock or wake-up call? Some of the hotel telephones have an obnoxious, loud ring that sounds more like a fire alarm: RING! RING! Half asleep, I reach for the phone and either drop it or start talking into the wrong end of the receiver.

I've checked the biblical record—Abraham never used an alarm clock. Not once. I've also read that most heart attacks occur before 9 a.m. Therefore, logically speaking, alarm clocks must cause heart attacks. Right! So, how do you prevent a heart attack? I figure, play it safe and stay in bed until 9:00 a.m.

One wake-up call I received on Sunday evening before the first day of my freshman year at Biola University was humorous for everyone but me. My home-away-from-home parents, John and Virginia Parker, had graciously opened their home to college students. Their beautiful home became a mini-college dorm for five of us. I wanted to start things off with a great night of sleep, so I went to bed at 9:30 p.m. The other coeds in our mini-dorm were out having fun, but not me. I left a note for my roommate, Bob Thune, to wake me at 5:30 a.m., slid between the sheets and was soon asleep.

At about 10:30 that evening, Bob and the others came home. He saw my request for a 5:30 a.m. wake-up and decided to have some fun. He cued the others into the plan, reset the clocks to 5:20 and the alarm for 5:30 a.m. Bob jumped into bed and waited for the alarm. RING! RING! I heard the alarm, but I sure didn't want to get up. Finally, I made it to my feet, and Bob asked, "How you feeling, Dave? Did you get a good night of sleep?"

"Great! Sure glad I went to bed early." I felt strangely groggy—like I had been drugged or something—but it's dark at 5:30 in the morning so I had no clue it was 10:45 p.m. Little did I realize I had slept a little more than an hour.

The others were going through the motions of getting ready for school—shaving, showering, blow drying their hair, getting dressed. Finally, I was set for my first day of college … at 11 p.m. I went downstairs to read my Bible—and everyone else went to bed.

Everything seemed normal until the front door opened. The Parkers came in … wearing the same clothes they had on the night before! My mind was spinning. Had they been out all night? Astounded, I asked, "Where have you been?"

"Oh, we've been over at the Rosses.'"

Wow, I thought, *all night … must have been an all-night prayer meeting.* They turned to go upstairs, and Virginia said, "See you in the morning!"

What? See you in the morning? And suddenly it hit me. I had been conned! I felt like the guy who stayed up all night to see where the sun went, and it finally dawned on him (bad pun, I know).

Picking up the story of Jonah, we read about his response to God's call on his life. The rebellious prophet decided to run from God. Not too bright! Rather than going to Nineveh as commanded, Jonah went the opposite direction to Tarshish, a city of great wealth (Ps. 72:10; Jer. 10:9; Ezek. 27:12, 25).

Though there is some question about the location, Herodotus, a Greek historian, identifies Tarshish with a city in southern Spain. Tarshish was a Phoenician port founded by a Carthaginian colony— the western most destination of Tyrian sailors. The area has been called "the Peru of Tyrian adventure" because it abounded in gold and silver mines.[24] For the record: Nineveh is 524 miles east of Joppa, Israel, Tarshish is about 2250 miles west as shown on the map. Jonah, behaving like a Nazi war criminal who seeks the most remote place on earth to hide after the war, selected the farthest port, the most remote place to escape in the known world.

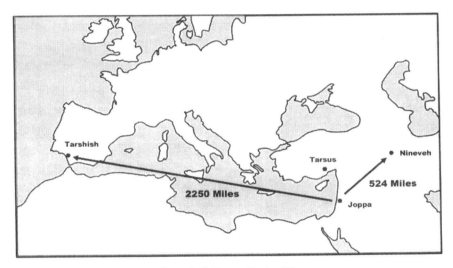

Jonah Attempts to Flee

Adapted from Michael Ramsay

---

24. *Easton's Illustrated Bible Dictionary* (WordSearch Corp., 2008), s.v. "Tarshish."

Did Jonah really think he could run away from God? Apparently so. After boarding the ship, the prophet fell sound asleep and was desperately in need of a wake-up call—physically and spiritually.

JONAH TOSSING IN HIS SLEEP

> The LORD hurled a great wind on the sea and there was a great storm on the sea so that the ship was about to break up. Then the sailors became afraid and every man cried to his god, and they threw the cargo which was in the ship into the sea to lighten it for them. But Jonah had gone below into the hold of the ship, lain down and fallen sound asleep. (Jonah 1:4–5)

The picture of Jonah "tossing in his sleep" gives new meaning to the phrase. His restlessness was more like lurching in his sleep. God hurls a "great storm" and a "great wind" on the ship and its crew. Four times in this chapter, we find the word "hurled" or "thrown" (Heb. *tul*): God hurls a storm upon them (v. 4), the cargo is hurled or thrown overboard (v. 5), and twice we read that Jonah is hurled or thrown overboard (vv. 12, 15). Clearly, God brought this storm, and the word "great" indicates a force at the extremes. This storm was so powerful that it threatened to break the ship into pieces.

Was this a hurricane? The biblical description certainly lends to that possibility. And a hurricane is far more dangerous over water than land. There are five categories of hurricanes according to this widely used scale.

Saffir-Simpson Hurricane Scale

Storm Category	Winds (mph)	Level of Damage	Storm Surge
1	74-95	MINIMAL: tears up vegetation, signs, power lines, heavy rain	4-5 ft.
2	96-110	MODERATE: tears off roofs, overturns small boats and mobile homes, flooding	6-8 ft.
3	111-130	EXTENSIVE: small buildings overturned, windows shattered, flooding of low-lying roads	9-12 ft.
4	131-155	EXTREME: trees down, roofs destroyed, homes destroyed, major flooding	13-18 ft.
5	155- +	CATASTROPHIC: most buildings destroyed, trees and plants uprooted, major flooding	18 ft. +

(Information from the National Hurricane Center)

Since this is a "great storm" with a "great wind," I think this may be a hurricane category 3, 4, or 5. If so, this small ship may have been lurching with swells ten to eighteen feet high and winds of 110 to 150 mph. Hurricane Katrina (Aug. 23–31, 2005) shocked us with its devastation and destruction. Reaching a wind speed of 175 mph, the storm claimed at least 1,245 lives. A modern cruise ship won't sail in a hurricane. If you've seen the dramatic movie *The Perfect Storm* based on events in Newfoundland, you have an idea of the terror at sea in a hurricane. In fact, this was God's "perfect storm" to confront a rebellious prophet with his defiance.

Whatever the category of the storm, total panic gripped the sailors, and each cried to his god while throwing cargo overboard to lighten the ship.

While the storm is awesome, there is something else even more amazing. Jonah was sleeping through it. *How could Jonah sleep in the hold of the ship with a storm raging and tossing the ship about like a rubber ducky going down a waterfall?* Maybe God zoned him out so deeply he was oblivious to the storm, or, and I think this is a possibility, Jonah was stone drunk. Was he attempting to quiet his conscience by drinking himself into a stupor? While the text does not say so, I have a hard time imagining how he could sleep through this storm without being heavily inebriated or supernaturally put into a deep sleep by God.

JONAH'S WAKE-UP CALL

With Jonah sound asleep in the ship and oblivious to the raging sea, it is time for a wake-up call.

> So the captain approached him and said, "How is it that you are sleeping? Get up, call on your god. Perhaps your god will be concerned about us so that we will not perish."
>
> Each man said to his mate, "Come, let us cast lots so we may learn on whose account this calamity has struck us." So they cast lots and the lot fell on Jonah. Then they said to him, "Tell us, now! On whose account has this calamity struck us? What is your occupation? And where do you come from? What is your country? From what people are you?" He said to them, "I am a Hebrew, and I fear the LORD God of heaven who made the sea and the dry land." (Jonah 1:6-9)

I picture the captain shaking the sleepy-eyed prophet—maybe a slap across the face or a douse of water—and screaming at him. "How can you sleep? … Get up and pray to your God! Maybe he will pay attention to us and spare our lives" (Jonah 1:6 NLT).

This is not Jonah's first wake-up call. The word "arise, get up, or wake up" is the Hebrew word *qum*, and it is used three times as a wake-up call for Jonah. This the first wake-up call: "Get up and go to the great city of Nineveh" (Jonah 1:2 NLT). The second one is from the captain of the ship who shakes Jonah and says, "Get up and pray to your god!" (v. 6). The third wake-up call was after Jonah was vomited out of the fish, "Get up and go to the great city of Nineveh, and deliver the message I have given you" (Jonah 3:2 NLT).

Once awake, Jonah begins to realize what a mess he is in. On deck, the crew decides to cast lots to determine the person responsible for the storm. The lot falls on Jonah. Was this chance, divination, or God's direction? Casting lots was commonly used and probably involved putting each name on a wood chip and drawing one out or something similar.[25]

Proverbs reminds us that God controls every throw of the lot and uses it to accomplish his purpose: "The lot is cast into the lap, but its every decision is from the LORD" (Prov. 16:33).

---

25. The casting of lots appears over seventy times in the Bible. In some cases, casting lots was a method to make a fair, objective decision—something like flipping a coin. The soldiers cast lots while Jesus hung on the cross to determine who would receive his clothing (Matt. 27:35). The casting of lots was used to divide the land of Canaan (Josh. 14:2). Casting lots was also used to settle disputes (Prov. 18:18). Proverbs 16:33 affirms that the Lord controls the outcome of the cast lot. At other times, casting lots was a procedure to determine divine guidance. They cast lots in a process of elimination to determine the guilt of Achan (Josh. 7:14–18). In the New Testament, the remaining disciples prayed and cast lots to select Mathias (Acts 1:26). Biblical qualifications (1 Tim. 3; Titus 1), prayer and fasting (Acts 14:23) are God's method to choose church leaders now that the Holy Spirit has been given—not the casting of lots (Dave Beckwith).

JONAH'S REQUEST FOR ASSISTED SUICIDE

> Then the men became extremely frightened and they said to him, "How could you do this?" For the men knew that he was fleeing from the presence of the LORD, because he had told them. So they said to him, "What should we do to you that the sea may become calm for us?"—for the sea was becoming increasingly stormy. He said to them, "Pick me up and throw me into the sea. Then the sea will become calm for you, for I know that on account of me this great storm has come upon you." However, the men rowed desperately to return to land but they could not, for the sea was becoming even stormier against them. Then they called on the LORD and said, "We earnestly pray, O LORD, do not let us perish on account of this man's life and do not put innocent blood on us; for You, O LORD, have done as You have pleased."
> (Jonah 1:10-14)

Anyone thrown into this turbulent sea would expect to die. I can't imagine that Jonah had any thought of being swallowed by a fish or being rescued. But rather than jumping over, he requests that the crew participate in his suicide. Why didn't Jonah jump and commit suicide on his own? As a prophet, Jonah knew the teaching and strong warnings prohibiting suicide. Both Moses (Num. 11:15) and Elijah (1 Kings 19:4), in times of great despondency, requested that God take their life—but never would they think of taking their own life. His convictions regarding suicide likely prevented him from taking his life.

It's amazing that these rugged sailors didn't pick Jonah up and throw him into the sea without a second thought. It's even more amazing that these sailors had more concern for Jonah than Jonah had for the thousands of lost people in Nineveh.

The storm continued to rage and grew even more violent. The sailors cried out to God asking forgiveness and pleading that they not be held responsible for taking the life of Jonah. Finally, they threw Jonah overboard, and the raging sea grew quiet. Wow! You could almost hear their gasp of astonishment. Remember when Jesus "… rebuked the wind and said to the sea, 'Hush, be still.' And the wind died down and it became perfectly calm" (Mk. 4:39). This is the same miracle.

THE SAILORS' WAKE-UP CALL

> Then the men feared the LORD greatly, and they offered a sacrifice to the LORD and made vows. And the LORD appointed a great fish to swallow Jonah, and Jonah was in the stomach of the fish three days and three nights.
> (Jonah 1:16–17)

The sailors were in complete awe at what had taken place. They repented—offering sacrifices and making vows. When they returned to shore, I think they made some amends with people they had cheated or hurt, wives they may have been unfaithful to, or children they had neglected. They were changed men. They met the Living God who calmed a raging storm. Jesus still calms storms. He can calm the storms in your life.

The phrase, "God provided a fish," means to "appoint" as in a divine appointment. God commissioned a fish to do his will, and the fish didn't swim for Tarshish. Smart fish! The fish was smarter than Jonah and more obedient.

It was one thing for Jonah to survive in the stomach of the fish; it was quite another for that fish to stomach Jonah. What a tummy ache that fish must have had with a hard-headed prophet banging around inside.

THIS IS YOUR WAKE-UP CALL

On the day of the Los Angeles earthquake, February 9, 1971, our chapel speaker at Talbot School of Theology told this humorous and thought-provoking story. The Lord had convicted him about getting up early to have his quiet time. He determined he would get up at 5:45 a.m. for devotions. The alarm went off at 5:45 a.m., and he reached over and turned it off. At 5:50, his wife came to wake him and remind him of his commitment. He rolled over and went back to sleep. At 5:55 a.m., the earth began to shake, the closet doors began to swing, and he came flying out of bed saying, "Lord, anything you want."

Don't wait for an earthquake or hurricane to wake you up spiritually. As Paul said, "So then let us not sleep as others do but let us be alert and sober. For those who sleep do their sleeping at night, and those who get drunk get drunk at night. But since we are of the day, let us be sober, having put on the breastplate of faith and love, and as a helmet, the hope of salvation" (1 Thess. 5:6–8).

God still gives wake-up calls. As Jonah experienced, the storms of life howl while many are fast asleep. "Be alert and sober" (v. 6). In other words, don't be intoxicated, don't be stoned, don't be spaced out—this is not God's will for your life (Eph. 5:17–18). To the church in Sardis, Jesus said, "Wake up! Strengthen what little remains, for even what is left is almost dead. I find that your actions do not meet the requirements of my God. Go back to what you heard and believed at first; hold to it firmly. Repent and turn to me again. If you don't wake up, I will come to you suddenly, as unexpected as a thief" (Rev. 3:2–3 NLT).

Here are four practical tips to be spiritually awake.

First, don't pull the covers over your head.

You can't run from your problems, and you certainly can't run from God. Healthy people don't run from their problems. God knows where you're at, he knows what you're avoiding, and he knows your heart. God had GPS (global positioning service) long before it was invented and put into practice in the 1980s and 90s. I call God's GPS God's People Scan. "The eyes of the LORD search the whole earth in order to strengthen those whose hearts are fully committed to him" (2 Chron. 16:9 NLT). God scans the planet seeing far more than any GPS device. He sees those who have their hearts turned against him as well as those sound asleep spiritually. God's GPS also identifies those who love him and are fully committed to him—and he infuses them with his strength.

God says, "Awake, O sleeper, rise up from the dead, and Christ will give you light" (Eph. 5:14 NLT). Don't pull a Rip Van Winkle—he was escaping from his problems, playing ninepins, drinking ale, and snoozing for twenty years. Life quickly passes. Be the person God wants you to be one day at a time. Don't wait for a tragedy to wake you up.

"Gary has been shot!" Shirley shouted as she came running into the worship center before church services began. Gary and Shirley Wilson had been legally separated for about a year and a half due to his gambling addiction. We prayed for Gary that morning in all the services. Later we heard what had happened.

At 1:20 a.m. in a gang-infested area of Tucson, Arizona, Gary unloaded three new Mazda cars from his eighteen-wheeler. While in a dark hallway outside the dealership, Gary looked up and saw two masked gang members approaching him. One gangbanger raised a double-barreled shotgun and fired, hitting Gary in the groin area and right leg. Gary hobbled outside and collapsed on the pavement wearing only his shorts—his pants had been blown off by the shotgun blast. A neighbor across the street heard the shot and called for an ambulance. Gary was rushed to the hospital where doctors performed surgery. He was placed under protective security keeping his identity out of the hospital computer. Police concluded the attack was a gang initiation and feared the gang members might return to the hospital to complete the task of killing Gary. The shooter and his accomplice were never apprehended.

About four years earlier, Gary and Shirley, along with their family, started attending Woodbridge Community Church in Irvine where I served as senior pastor. We embraced them and attempted to help them out with their financial needs. Strangely, they seemed to be out of money every few weeks even though Gary had a good job as a trucker, and Shirley worked in the church preschool.

One day I got a tip: "Gary has a gambling problem!" His truck route took him through Las Vegas where he was blowing money at the slot machines and blackjack table. This explained where all the money was going. The next time I saw Gary, I confronted him with his gambling problem. He vehemently denied having a problem and exploded as he stormed out of my office.

Gary disappeared for a year and a half. He and Shirley were legally separated due to his gambling. No one knew where he was, including his family. We later learned Gary was living in his big rig and gambling away what money he earned.

After the shooting, Gary was released from the hospital and transported back to Orange County in California. I went over to the house where he was staying—not knowing what to expect after our last explosive confrontation. I knocked on the screen door, and he invited me in. When Gary saw me, he burst into a flood of tears. "You're right, pastor. I have a big gambling problem. I've been blowing about $2000 a month gambling."

"Gary, this is your special day," I responded. "God has spared your life and wants you to surrender your life to him." Struggling to get to his knees with the gunshot wounds, Gary knelt with me in prayer and surrendered his life to Christ.

A short time later, Gary and Shirley renewed their wedding vows before the church. Gary bought a special ring for Shirley and presented it to her that day. Their marriage had been salvaged and restored. Today their love and respect for each other is beautiful, and their marriage has never been stronger.

Gary told me recently, "Pastor, don't take this wrong, but I'm glad I was shot. I would have never come to the end of myself and stopped ruining my life and family with gambling. I haven't gambled even once since that day in 2003."

I replied, "Gary, I'm glad you were shot because it brought you to Christ. Your life has been transformed, and your family restored."

Second, open your eyes and pray for those who make your life difficult.

When you wake up in the morning, who pops into your mind that makes your life difficult? They may be bad-tempered, vindictive, or malicious. You may be dreading the day because you know you will face them. Begin your day by praying for them. This is what Jesus said to do: "Love your enemies and pray for those who persecute you" (Matt. 5:44). Ask God for insight into their behavior and an opportunity to surprise them with love and kindness.

Third, wake up and smell the coffee.

Paul, recognizing the urgency of the hour, issues this wake-up call for every believer, "Do this, knowing the time, that it is already the hour for you to awaken from sleep; for now salvation is nearer to us than when we believed. The night is almost gone, and the day is near. Therefore, let us lay aside the deeds of darkness and put on the armor of light" (Rom. 13:11-12).

Time is running out. Peter wrote, "The Lord is not slow in doing what he promised—the way some people understand slowness" (2 Peter 3:9 NCV). God doesn't keep time the way you and I do. God isn't looking at some cosmic clock wringing his hands and worried that things are running behind schedule. God is never late. Why the delay? "God is being patient with you. He does not want anyone to be lost, but he wants all people to change their hearts and lives" (2 Pet. 3:9 NCV). God is waiting for that last person to repent, wake-up, and receive him into their life before the end of all things.

> But the day of the Lord will come like a thief, in which the heavens will pass away with a roar and the elements will be destroyed with intense heat, and the earth and its works will be burned up.
>
> Since all these things are to be destroyed in this way, what sort of people ought you to be in holy conduct and godliness, looking for and hastening the coming of the day of God, because of which the heavens will be destroyed by burning, and the elements will melt with intense heat! (2 Peter 3:10–12)

The *Washington Post* carried this headline not long ago:

"The Doomsday Clock is ticking again. It is now three minutes to 'midnight,' a.k.a. the end of humanity."[26]

The world clock is not something conjured up by Christian alarmists. The world clock was created by scientists to assess the threat of the world ending. Periodically they look at wars and potential wars, the proliferation of nuclear weapons, population explosion, ecological threats, famine, the spread of disease, and other factors to set the clock indicating how much time until the world ends. Now, with the added proliferation of information warfare, the *Bulletin of Atomic Scientists* moved the clock to *two minutes* to 'midnight" as of January 2019.[27]

Fourth, get up and get dressed.

"Look, I will come as unexpectedly as a thief! Blessed are all who are watching for me, who keep their clothing ready so they will not have to walk around naked and ashamed." (Rev. 16:15 NLT)

So remove your dark deeds like dirty clothes, and put on the shining armor of right living. Because we belong to the day, we must live decent lives for all to see.

Don't participate in the darkness of wild parties and drunkenness, or in sexual promiscuity and immoral living, or in quarreling and jealousy. Instead, clothe

26. Abby Ohlheiser, *The Washington Post,* Jan. 22, 2015, accessed Mar. 31, 2019, https://www.washingtonpost.com/news/speaking-of-science/wp/2015/01/22/the-doomsday-clock-is-ticking-again-it-is-now-three-minutes-to-midnight-a-k-a-the-end-of-humanity/?noredirect=on&utm_term=.9d43774bba1f.
27. "Press Release: Welcome to 'The New Abnormal,'" *Bulletin of Atomic Scientists,* Jan. 24, 2019, accessed Mar. 31, 2019, https://thebulletin.org/2019/01/press-release-welcome-to-the-new-abnormal/.

yourself with the presence of the Lord Jesus Christ. And don't let yourself think about ways to indulge your evil desires. (Rom. 13:12–14 NLT)

Put on the character of the Lord Jesus. Let your light shine with the fruit of the Spirit: love, joy, peace, patience, kindness, goodness, faithfulness, gentleness, and self-control.

While in high school, I memorized this motto from a church wall in Kansas City, Missouri. It has become a reminder and goal for my life.

WAKE UP,

SING UP,

PREACH UP,

PRAY UP,

PAY UP,

STAY UP,

AND NEVER GIVE UP,

LET UP,

BACK UP,

OR SHUT UP,

UNTIL THE CAUSE OF CHRIST

IN MY LIFE,

MY CHURCH,

MY COMMUNITY,

AND THE WORLD IS BUILT UP.[28]

---

28. Roy B. Zuck, *The Speaker's Quote Book: Over 5,000 Illustrations and Quotations for All Occasions, Revised and Expanded* (Grand Rapids, MI: Kregel Publications, 2009), 560.

TIME OUT

CHAPTER TWO

THIS IS YOUR WAKE-UP CALL

"Wake up! Strengthen what little remains, for even what is left is almost dead. I find that your actions do not meet the requirements of my God. Go back to what you heard and believed at first; hold to it firmly. Repent and turn to me again. If you don't wake up, I will come to you suddenly, as unexpected as a thief." (Rev. 3:2–3 NLT)

GROW AND APPLY

◊ Read Jonah 1:4–17.

◊ If the "great storm" with the "great wind" that threatened to break the ship into pieces was a hurricane, what category of hurricane do you think it was?

_____

_____

_____

_____

_____

_____

◊ Describe a storm you've been in like a hurricane, flood, blizzard, earthquake, tornado or some other life-threatening situation. Did you experience sheer panic? If so, what was it like?

_____

_____

_____

_____

_____

God's GPS

GOD'S PEOPLE SCAN

The eyes of the LORD search the whole earth in order to strengthen those whose hearts are fully committed to him. (2 Chron. 16:9 NLT)

◊ Imagine you're looking into the screen of God's GPS. What does God see as he scans the billions of people on planet earth?

_____

_____

_____

_____

_____

_____

◊ What does God see as he scans your heart?

_____

_____

_____

_____

_____

◊ To sharpen the focus as to what God sees, read Psalm 139:1–4:

> O LORD, you have examined my heart and know everything about me. You know when I sit down or stand up. You know my thoughts even when I'm far away. You see me when I travel and when I rest at home. You know everything I do. You know what I am going to say even before I say it, LORD. (Ps. 139:1–4 NLT)

PRAY

Pray through the words of Psalm 139:1–4 for your life. As you're allowing the Holy Spirit to inspect your life, pray (or sing if you know the song) the words to a children's song from years ago.

Be careful little eyes what you see (repeat twice),
For the Father up above is looking done with love,
So be careful little eyes what you see.
Several verses follow:
Be careful little ears what you hear.
Be careful little mouth what you say.
Be careful little feet where you go.
Be careful little hands what you do.

SHARE

People often talk about the weather so strike up a conversation about the weather. Here are a few thought-provoking questions to take the subject further.

1. What is the worst storm you've experienced? Tornado, hurricane, earthquake, flood, blizzard, etc.
2. Did you pray during that storm?
3. What prompts you to pray today?

TIME TOGETHER

CHAPTER TWO

THIS IS YOUR WAKE-UP CALL

If you're leading a small group, teaching a Bible class, or sharing with the family, below are some opening questions. For the content of the lesson, use the Grow and Apply, Prayer, and Share sections with your Time Out.

CONNECT
(choose one or two for discussion)

◊ What do you look like when the morning alarm rings? What do you feel like?

_____

_____

_____

_____

_____

_____

◊ Are you a morning person? Or a night owl? Or neither?

_____

_____

_____

_____

_____

_____

◊ When have you experienced a "life wake-up call"?

_____

_____

_____

_____

_____

_____

CHAPTER THREE

A WHALE OF A TALE?

I've been deep-sea fishing only once. Once was enough. Little did I know how close I was to being "pastor overboard."

"Deep-sea fishing is a man thing," my friend Pastor Roy McBeth said. "It's a great way to relate to other men." I signed up. Early on the morning of February 3, 1986, I joined seven or eight men from the church as we boarded the 65-foot *Merry Jane* charter fishing boat departing from Bodega Bay Harbor, about an hour north of San Francisco.

Once we arrived at a good fishing spot, I dropped my line and waited to see if I would catch something. Soon my line seemed to be caught on something—perhaps the rocks at the bottom of the ocean. I reeled the line out a little and then started to bring it back in. Suddenly, I realized I had something big on my line putting up a ferocious fight. Sweating and straining, I was sure my rod and reel would break ... or I'd lose my grip, and this fish would spend its remaining days with a rod and reel in its mouth. I kept reeling it in, and finally, fighting and leaping, a great white shark surfaced. Knowing I was an amateur, the captain came over to help, lifting my catch up and over the side of the ship and onto the deck. What a sight! To my amazement, I bagged the prize for catching the biggest fish that day—a 6-foot, 159-pound great white shark. This was long before the great white shark was protected by the Endangered Species Act in 2013.

On the return trip, I was horribly seasick. Why had I brought a sack lunch? I couldn't stand the thought of food. I had wondered why the other guys didn't bring their lunches—now I knew why. With the boat bucking powerful waves and tilting thirty to forty degrees, I was desperately hanging on. No life jackets had been distributed. The *Merry Jane* was sailing directly into huge waves, and the little craft was lurching and heaving wildly. I was praying—fearful of being thrown overboard. Spotting dry land was a huge relief.

A few days later, on Saturday, February 8, I opened the Santa Rosa *Press Democrat* to see a picture of the *Merry Jane*. After a fifteen-foot wave crashed into the boat's stern, the *Merry Jane* turned ninety degrees on its side, and nineteen passengers were swept into the frigid waters. Amazingly, the boat didn't capsize. Two patrol boats, a coast guard helicopter, and the eighty-two-foot cutter *Point Chino* and a shore crew searched desperately for the missing people. Late on Sunday, the coast guard called off its search knowing the fifty-five-degree water rapidly causes hypothermia. Nine people perished.[29]

The captain of the *Merry Jane* was charged with negligence and manslaughter for taking an illegal return route to save time.

29. "Search Called Off for 4 Still Missing From Boat," *Los Angeles Times*, February 10, 1986, from United Press International; "Make Preservers a Must, Panel Says," *Los Angeles Times,* September 17, 1986, United Press International; "Marine casualty report: fishing vessel Merry Jane, O.N. 596815, broaching on 8 February 1986 approaching Bodega Bay, California between Bodega Head and Bodega Rock with multiple loss of life and injuries to passengers," United States Coast Guard, Marine Board of Investigation.

He had steered the ship between Bodega Head and Bodega Rock—a dangerous path among jagged rocks. Because of this incident, the National Transportation Safety Board urged the coast guard to require that passengers on small sea-going vessels wear life preservers when their boats enter or leave ports where they might encounter high waves.

God protected me and spared my life.

A BIG FISH STORY

When someone says, "Now that's a whale of a tale," it implies a tale bigger than life—something awesome, enormous, incredible. The phrase, "a whale of a tale," may owe its origin to this big daddy of all fish stories: Jonah being swallowed by a fish and living to tell about it. Is this story fact or fiction? A miracle or a myth?

The testimony of Jesus affirms Jonah's experience in the fish as a factual miracle, but the book of Jonah also records, not just one miracle, but twelve.

1. God hurls a great wind and storm on the sea (1:4).
2. God uses the casting of lots to identify Jonah (1:7).
3. God abruptly calms the storm (1:15).
4. God brings about the conversion of the sailors (1:16).
5. God appoints a great fish to swallow Jonah at the right moment (1:17).
6. God protects Jonah as he is eaten and swallowed by the great fish (1:17).
7. God keeps Jonah alive inside the fish for three days and nights (1:17).
8. God commands the fish to vomit Jonah onto dry land (2:10).

9. God brings about the conversion of the great city of Nineveh (3:10).
10. God appoints a plant to grow (4:6).
11. God appoints the worm (4:7).
12. God appoints the scorching east wind (4:8).

If you believe God created the universe, you need no further evidence. Miracles are the stuff God does. The greatest miracle in the book was the conversion of the sailors and the city of Nineveh. Calming storms, arranging for a fish to swallow a stubborn prophet, and preserving his life are finger-work miracles for God. Easy stuff. The greatest miracle, then and now, is God changing a hardened heart and transforming a human life.

On the other hand, critics have more difficulty swallowing these miraculous events than the fish had swallowing Jonah. They have invented fanciful tales to explain away the supernatural. For example,

1. Jonah had a dream during his sleep on the ship, and the book of Jonah is the account of his dream;

2. The book of Jonah is related to the Phoenician myth of Hercules and the sea monster (similarity between the two accounts is nearly nonexistent);

3. Jonah suffered shipwreck on the way to Tarshish and was rescued by another ship that had a fish for its emblem; or

4. During a storm, Jonah took refuge in a dead fish that was floating around.[30]

---

30. McGee, *Thru the Bible*, 737.

Wild! Add your own fish story if you like. One fish story smells as fishy as the next. After reading these silly speculations, the actual account is remarkably believable.

WHAT KIND OF WHALE OR FISH SWALLOWED JONAH?

> The LORD appointed a great fish to swallow Jonah, and Jonah was in the stomach of the fish three days and three nights. (Jonah 1:17)

> For as Jonah was in the belly of the great fish for three days and three nights, so will the Son of Man be in the heart of the earth for three days and three nights. (Matt. 12:40 NLT)

I like the quip of evangelist and pastor Greg Laurie: "Newsflash: Fish Bites Man. ... It's sort of like eating sushi in reverse. Instead of man-eating fish, we have a fish-eating man."[31]

Was the "great fish" that swallowed Jonah a species of fish or a whale? The Hebrew words used for "great fish" in Jonah 1:17 are *gadol* (meaning mega-sized) and *dawg* (referring generally to a fish). There is another word used elsewhere in the Old Testament, *tanniyn,* that refers to a serpent, a dragon, and a sea monster which probably included dinosaurs as well as creatures that live in the water (Gen. 1:21; Job 7:12); however, this is not the word used in Jonah. Dr. Warren Baker, general editor of the *Complete Word Study Dictionary* and former instructor of Hebrew and Old Testament studies at Faith Seminary, comments regarding this word "fish" (Heb. *dawg*).

31. Greg Laurie, *A Fresh Look at the Book of Jonah* (Kerygma Publishers, 2014), 9.

Jonah 1:17 tells us that God prepared a great fish. He, who can do anything, could have made the fish capable of swallowing Jonah, preserving him in its belly and then casting him out again alive. ... This term was in that day, as it is common parlance for any kind of aquatic creature. Its nontechnical usage would allow for a mammal such as a whale and would, therefore, contain no error.[32]

In Matthew 12:40, Jesus used the Greek word *ketos* sometimes translated "whale" or "sea monster" or "huge fish." A whale or a species of fish would meet the biblical criteria to be Jonah's submarine hotel in both the Old and New Testament.

If you're intrigued with the "how to" for this incredible miracle or perhaps a bit skeptical, consider these two possibilities for the fish or whale that swallowed Jonah.

BLUE WHALE?

Blue whales, the largest animal known to have lived, grow up to a hundred feet in length and weigh as much as 272,000 pounds. The following drawing illustrates the enormous size of the blue whale in comparison to an elephant.

---

32. *Complete Word Study Dictionary* (AMG Publisher, 1994), s.v. "Matt. 12:40: whale."

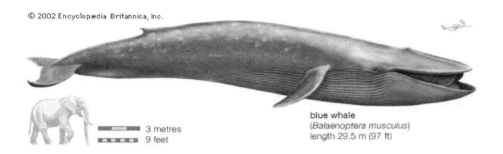

© 2002 Encyclopædia Britannica, Inc.

3 metres
9 feet

blue whale
(*Balaenoptera musculus*)
length 29.5 m (97 ft)

BLUE WHALE
Reproduced by permission from *Encyclopædia Britannica*
© 2002 by Encyclopædia Britannica, Inc.

According to the Blue Whale Project, the whale's tail is as wide as a professional soccer net (about twenty-five feet). They are warm-blooded creatures, and as mammals, they draw in air every five to fifteen minutes. When they exhale through their blowhole, the blow can reach thirty feet high and smells terrible. The arteries of Big Blue are about nine inches in diameter (or about the size of a dinner plate). When a dead blue whale washed ashore in Canada scientists finally got to see what the heart of the planet's largest animal looked like. The heart in this blue whale was nearly the size of a golf cart weighing in at about 400 pounds.[33]

Blue whales can communicate with other blue whales up to 2,000 miles away by utilizing a special layer of water where they

---

33. "See the World's Biggest Heart," *BBC,* Aug. 20, 2015, accessed Mar. 31, 2019, http://www.bbc.com/earth/story/20150820-see-the-worlds-biggest-heart-blue-whales-is-first-to-be-preserved.

send and receive messages. Scientists have discovered that the sound is channeled by a layer of low-density water above and a layer of high-density water below known as the Sound Fixing and Ranging channel—abbreviated SOFAR.[34]

The mouth of the blue whale is giant-sized extending all the way to their belly button, and their tongue is the size of an elephant. When they open their mouth, they swallow huge volumes of water or whatever else is in their path. The blue whale has accordion-like folds of skin that expand like a water balloon, big enough to hold 15,000 gallons of water. (This is more water than a back-yard swimming pool that is fifteen feet wide, thirty feet long, and four feet deep and holds 13,500 gallons of water). Blue whales do not bite their prey since they have no teeth. God designed them with fingernail-like plates called baleen—which is made from keratin, the same product God made fingernails from. The whale doesn't swallow the water. Instead, it forces most of the water out by shutting its mouth and forcing the water out through the baleen plates. Tons of krill (small shrimp-like crustaceans) get stuck in the baleen plates, and then the whale swallows them. The stomach of a blue whale can hold one ton of krill, and they may eat as much as four tons of food a day.

> Also, we know from the biblical account that Jonah sank to the depths of the ocean. Big blues dive deep before they come up to capture their prey. It is also believed that the whales need to take in large volumes of air to make such massive sounds. So Jonah would have had plenty of room, food, and air inside a big blue; and he would have had no large teeth to contend with.[35]

---

34. Dr. Joe Francis, "Big Blue Whales," *Answers Magazine,* July 1, 2011, accessed Mar. 31, 2019, https://answersingenesis.org/aquatic-animals/big-blue/.

35. Francis, "Big Blue Whales," *Answers Magazine,* July 1, 2011, accessed Mar. 31, 2019, https://answersingenesis.org/aquatic-animals/big-blue/

There are several accounts of whales and sharks swallowing human beings with the victim living to tell about it. However, the further you dig checking the facts, the more "fishy" the stories become. Perhaps future research will produce the evidence to validate the stories, but until then it is best to consider them as intriguing fish stories but not actual events.

There is another strong possibility for the sea creature that swallowed Jonah.

GOLIATH GROUPER FISH?

Groupers are part of the large and varied bass fish family called *Serranidae* consisting of about 400 species. Groupers live in tropical and temperate seas all over the world and grow up to twelve feet in length and weigh as much as 1,000 pounds.[36] Angler Lynn Joyner reeled in a 680-pound goliath grouper on May 20, 1961, at Fernandina Beach, Florida.

GOLIATH GROUPER FISH

Wikipedia Encyclopedia

The goliath grouper is noted for its huge mouth and jaw that are like an underwater sweeper capable of suctioning in the food

---

36. John E. Randall, *Caribbean Reef Fishes* (Neptune City, N.J: T.F.H. Publications, 1968), 57.

it wants—including man—in one enormous gulp.[37] The mouth of the grouper has a powerful sucking system that sucks prey in from a distance.[38] Chris Koenig, a retired University of Florida marine biologist who has studied goliaths for decades, was quoted in *National Geographic*, "The longest teeth in their mouth are an eighth of an inch. Sure, they are sharp, but you have to provoke them, and then the worst they can do is give you a rash. Sharks will take your hand off. Goliath suck their prey, they have such a weak bite."[39] Jonah could have been swallowed by suction without being hurt by the teeth of a goliath grouper.

The stomachs of goliath groupers have been found to contain an incredible assortment of large and small creatures and objects. This enormous fish "… has been known to stalk pearl divers and shell divers the way a cat stalks a mouse and has been recorded as rushing a diver in an apparent attack. It is the basis of stories of skin divers being swallowed by giant groupers."[40]

In 1990, groupers were identified as an endangered species, but now they are returning in significant numbers. *National Geographic* published an article entitled, "800-Pound Groupers Making a Comeback—But Not Everyone's Happy." The goliath

37. Buddy Davis and Kay Davis, "Grouper," *Answers Magazine,* Jan. 18, 2016, accessed Mar. 31, 2019, .https://answersingenesis.org/kids/fish/grouper/.

38. *Wikipedia Encyclopedia, the Free Encyclopedia*, s.v. "Grouper," accessed Mar. 31, 2019, https://en.wikipedia.org/wiki/Grouper.

39. Laura Parker, "800-Pound Groupers Making a Comeback—But Not Everyone's Happy," *National Geographic*, Nov. 25, 2016, accessed April 20, 2019, https://news.nationalgeographic.com/2016/11/groupers-oceans-goliath-fishing/.

40. Bernard L. Gordon, *The Secret Lives of Fishes* (New York: Grosset & Dunlap, 1977), 193.

groupers gobble the fish off the lines of fishermen. Brice Barr, a charter boat skipper and president of the Key West Charter Fishermen's Association, said, "The goliaths will catch every single fish that you hook. They hear the sound of our boats and that's the dinner bell. They know they are going to get fed."[41]

The *National Geographic* article also included a link to a video showing a grouper dragging a fisherman and stealing his catch. You can find many other fascinating videos of groupers on *YouTube*.

Groupers are adept at changing color patterns to blend into their background. They may disappear into coral with brown bands and blue body and emerge from the other side in brilliant yellow with black dots.[42]

Groupers (along with their close relatives the giant sea bass) have been called jewfish for centuries. Since the groupers have scales and fins, they are clean fish according to Levitical law. Hence the name jewfish. The name was changed from jewfish to goliath grouper in 2001 because of complaints that the name was anti-Semitic. Do you think God used a jewfish to swallow a stubborn Jewish prophet?

Scientists are exploring another fascinating feature of the goliath grouper. These enormous fish are territorial and make low-frequency "booms" when divers approach. Researchers believe the boom is a distress call issued in response to intruders, including military movements such as submarines and underwater drones. A research effort called Persistent Aquatic

---

41. Parker, "800-Pound Groupers Making a Comeback" https:// news.nationalgeographic.com/2016/11/groupers-oceans-goliath-fish-ing/.

42. Davis and Davis, "Grouper," *Answers Magazine*, Jan. 18, 2016, accessed Mar. 31, 2019, https://answersingenesis.org/kids/fish/grouper/.

Living Sensors (PALS) is exploring the possibility of the goliath grouper being an underwater surveillance system capable of detecting an enemy's underwater vehicles, drones, and large submarines.[43]

My friend Wayne Brown, a marine biologist, has spent most of his adult life studying the creatures in the sea. He and his wife, Karen, swim with and photograph sharks as well as many other sea creatures. Their travels have taken them worldwide to study marine life. Wayne and Karen do public school assemblies with photographs and stories that awe their audiences and give glory to God the Creator.[44] As an underwater research expert, Wayne's study has led him to the conclusion that the grouper fish best fits the possibilities as the fish that swallowed Jonah.

The highly-respected research team with the *Undersea World of Jacques Cousteau* did a television special entitled "The Fish That Swallowed Jonah."[45] They concluded that the most likely fish to have swallowed Jonah was a variety of the grouper fish.

A significant portion of the program was devoted to an analysis of how this historic event took place. The biblical account was treated as factual and accurate as this scientific team examined every possibility of Jonah being swallowed, living in the stomach of the fish, and finally being ejected alive. The research of Wayne and Karen Brown concurs with the research of Jacques Cousteau.

---

43. Allie Wilkinson, "Military Tries Out Fish as Underwater Spies," *Scientific American* (Mar. 29, 2019), accessed on Mar. 31, 2019, www.scientificamerican.com/article/military-tries-out-fish-as-underwater-spies.

44. Contact Wayne and Karen Brown at The Ocean Adventure, accessed Mar. 31, 2019, http://www.theoceanadventure.com/bio.html.

45. "The Fish That Swallowed Jonah, Episode 36 of 37," *Jacques Cousteau Odyssey*, accessed Mar. 31, 2019, https://www.youtube.com/watch?v=k09tlo0ME5o, Aug. 7, 1988.

What kind of fish or whale swallowed Jonah? We'll never know for certain this side of heaven. Jonah and I are going to have a long conversation when I see him. It may have been a blue whale or goliath grouper fish or possibly another sea creature. But of this you can be certain: Jonah's rescue was an astounding miracle and happened just as recorded in the Bible.

WHAT DIFFERENCE DOES IT MAKE?

Skeptics may scoff and say, "It makes little difference whether Jonah and the fish is factual or an allegory." I'm astounded by Christians falling for this line of reasoning. It makes a big difference. Here's why.

First, it matters because the death and resurrection of Jesus matter.

If Jonah and the fish is nothing but a fanciful fish story, the death and resurrection of Jesus Christ is in question. Jesus said, "For as Jonah was in the belly of the great fish for three days and three nights, so will the Son of Man be in the heart of the earth for three days and three nights" (Matt. 12:40 NLT). The veracity of one account is related to the other. If we cannot believe Jesus regarding Jonah, how can we believe him when he says, "For God loved the world so much that he gave his one and only Son, so that everyone who believes in him will not perish but have eternal life" (John 3:16 NLT).

What about the reference to "three days and nights"? To our way of thinking, this means three 24-hour day periods of time, but Jewish thinking was different in this regard as noted by John MacArthur.

> "Three days and three nights" was an emphatic way of saying "three days," and by Jewish reckoning this would be an apt way of expressing a period of time that includes parts of 3 days. Thus, if Christ was crucified

on a Friday, and his resurrection occurred on the first day of the week, by Hebrew reckoning this would qualify as 3 days and 3 nights.[46]

A country doctor was called out to a farmer's home to deliver a baby. Following the birth, they realized they didn't have a scale to weigh the baby. The farmer's wife said, "How about that scale downstairs that you use to weigh your fish?" The farmer fetched the scale, and they weighed that newborn infant, and would you believe it? ... that baby weighed twenty-three pounds! Selah ... pause and calmly think about that! If the scale is off regarding the prophet and the fish, then the truthfulness regarding the baby, the Christ, and the resurrection are in question as well.

Second, it matters because we have no hope if it is not true.

If the death and resurrection of Jesus Christ are in question, our sins are unforgiven, our hope of life after death is in vain, and our faith is useless.

> If there is no resurrection of the dead, not even Christ has been raised; and if Christ has not been raised, then our preaching is vain, your faith also is vain. Moreover, we are even found to be false witnesses of God, because we testified against God that He raised Christ, whom He did not raise, if in fact the dead are not raised. For if the dead are not raised, not even Christ has been raised; and if Christ has not been raised, your faith is worthless; you are still in your sins. Then those also who have fallen asleep in Christ have perished. (1 Cor. 15:13–18)

---

46. John MacArthur, *The MacArthur Study Bible* (Thomas Nelson, Inc., 2006), 1383.

On the other hand, if Jonah was swallowed and spit out by that fish as the Bible says, the reliability of the Scriptures is affirmed. Sitting on a chair with a wobbly leg or two is not my idea of comfort or confidence. The account of Jonah and the fish is not only credible but stands the scrutiny of scientific investigation. Jonah and the fish are one of hundreds of foundational truths for your faith.

Third, it matters because *you* matter to God.

God was patient and loving with Jonah despite his rebellion, disobedience, and bigotry. God is patient and loving with you because you matter to him.

Let's imagine you flipped on your TV and heard a voice, "This is God. I want to show you all the times I spared your life." The video starts to play, and you're astounded and overwhelmed by the times God intervened to rescue you—times you didn't even know about. And then God says, "I want to show you all the times I have forgiven you when you've sinned and gone astray." The video plays on and on and on. You are driven to your knees with gratitude. Of course, this is imaginary on my part. God does not bring up our past failures. He has forgiven all our sins and chooses to remember them no more. "'I—yes, I alone—will blot out your sins for my own sake and will never think of them again'" (Isa. 43:25 NLT).

Since God sent Jesus to the cross to die for you and forgive your sins, you are important to him. And since God has spared your life and protected you, it matters that you are alive right now. Your next breath is a gift from God. Breathe deep of God's love and forgiveness. You're special to him.

TIME OUT

CHAPTER THREE

A WHALE OF A TALE?

The LORD appointed a great fish to swallow Jonah, and Jonah was in the stomach of the fish three days and three night. (Jonah 1:17)

For as Jonah was in the belly of the great fish for three days and three nights, so will the Son of Man be in the heart of the earth for three days and three nights. (Matt. 12:40 NLT)

GROW AND APPLY

◊ Read Psalm 107:1–31. This is a great Psalm with four pictures of deliverance.

1. Deliverance when lost (vv. 4–9);
2. Deliverance when imprisoned (vv. 10–16);

3. Deliverance when sick (vv. 17–22); and

4. Deliverance when tossing on a stormy sea (vv. 23–31). After each predicament, there is prayer and God's pardon. Finally, each section concludes with this verse of praise. "Let them praise the LORD for his great love and for the wonderful things he has done for them" (Ps. 107:8, 15, 21, 31 NLT).

◊ Now focus your attention on the fourth deliverance in vv. 23–31.

> Some went off to sea in ships, plying the trade routes of the world. They, too, observed the LORD's power in action, his impressive works on the deepest seas. He spoke, and the winds rose, stirring up the waves. Their ships were tossed to the heavens and plunged again to the depths; the sailors cringed in terror. They reeled and staggered like drunkards and were at their wits' end. "LORD, help!" they cried in their trouble, and he saved them from their distress. He calmed the storm to a whisper and stilled the waves. What a blessing was that stillness as he brought them safely into harbor! Let them praise the LORD for his great love and for the wonderful things he has done for them. (Ps. 107:23–31 NLT)

◊ What are the parallels in this psalm to the story of Jonah and the sailors?

_____

_____

_____

_____

_____

◊ What are the storms in your life? A frustrating situation? A difficult person? A medical issue? An emotional struggle?

_____

_____

_____

_____

_____

_____

◊ When have you gone the opposite direction from what God was wanting you to do?

_____

_____

_____

_____

_____

_____

PRAY

◊ Recount the times the Lord has delivered you. Has he delivered you when you were lost and confused? Set you free from the prison of sin? Healed you from a serious illness? Calmed the storm in a relationship?

_____

_____

_____

_____

_____

_____

After each thought of deliverance, respond in prayer: "I thank you God for your unfailing love and the wonderful things you have done for me."

_____

_____

_____

_____

_____

SHARE

A well-thought-through question often opens the door to share your faith. Most people have heard of the story of Jonah and the whale. Here are thought-provoking questions to ask when the time is right.

1. What do you think of when you hear the phrase, "Now that's a whale of a tale"?
2. Do you think it was a whale or a large fish that swallowed Jonah?
3. Who do you turn to when the storms of life come your way?

TIME TOGETHER

CHAPTER THREE

A WHALE OF A TALE?

If you're leading a small group, teaching a Bible class, or sharing with the family, below are some opening questions. For the content of the lesson, use the Grow and Apply, Prayer, and Share sections with your Time Out.

CONNECT
(choose one or two discussion questions)

◊ What was your favorite "hide out" when you were growing up?

_____

_____

_____

_____

◊ Tell about a time when you disobeyed your mom or dad or someone else. What were the consequences?

_____

_____

_____

_____

_____

CHAPTER FOUR

CHECKIN' INTO REHAB

What was living in a fish or a whale like? A Sunday school drawing from years ago pictured Jonah sitting at a table sipping lemonade and writing his upcoming message series for the Ninevites. Hah!

Hilarious and delightful is the children's story of Pinocchio and Geppetto inside "Monstro, the whale." They decided to build a fire so the smoke would tickle the whale's throat and cause the creature to have an enormous sneeze that would set them free.

Let's get real. Jonah's experience of being swallowed by a large fish or whale must have been terrifying beyond comprehension. In the novel, *The Paranoid Prophet,* William Backus describes Jonah telling his terrifying experience to his psychologist. While imaginative, it is probably not far from Jonah's actual experience.

> A sea creature, the size of a ship, was racing toward me, its mouth open. Screaming in terror, I was swallowed whole.
>
> I managed to breathe by keeping my head above the acidic fluids in the creature's gut. The stench was so overpowering I argued with myself before I drew each breath. Finally, I decided to inhale through my mouth, but the sour fumes hurt my lungs.

The darkness was total, "…" The noise all around me was like that of a huge machine. The thud of the creature's heartbeat, the swish of blood, the body fluids, and bubbling gasses hummed around me, hurting my ears. I knew nothing but terror.

My recollections from this point on are cloudy. It was as though I was buried alive—in hell without having died—and nothing could get me out. Terror overwhelmed my anger, and desperately I called out to God—even though, only a few hours before, I wanted to escape him forever.[47]

Here's a good summary of the book of Jonah:

"God said, 'Go.'

Jonah said, 'No.'

And God said, 'Oh?'"[48]

This is "God's 'Oh? You think you're in control of your life? Oh? You think you can defy me? Oh? You think you can hide from me? Oh?'" Mike Howerton, writing in *Glorious Mess*, said, "Let's personalize what we see in Jonah's life: when we are not right with God, storms are everywhere. When we run from God, relationships stop working, friendships are shallow, family life is sticky, the future seems unclear and stormy. Your personal attitude is in a shaky place, so you have to try to distract yourself and find false substitutes to make yourself feel better. You are running from God's best."[49]

This is rehab for Jonah. We all need rehab—it's not just for alcoholics and druggies. With enduring love, God leads us through rehab—though it may not be in a facility. It may

---

47. William Backus, *The Paranoid Prophet* (Minneapolis: Bethany House Publishers, 1986), 64.

48. Laurie, *A Fresh Look,* 11.

49. Mike Howerton, *Glorious Mess* (Grand Rapids, MI: Baker Books, 2012), 70.

be when you're at the end of your hope rope! Tragedy has hit. You feel abandoned, beyond the loving arms of God. You're in constant turmoil. You're lower than a whale's belly. Panic seems to strangle you.

Take heart. Being at your lowest may be the best thing that ever happened to you.

WHEN YOU'RE AT YOUR LOWEST …
1. God isn't as distant as you think.

Have you ever felt God abandoned you? You're sinking in unpaid bills or drowning in despair. Angry people are making your life miserable. The one you love has left you. Everything seems upside down, and you're not sure which side is up. Before you conclude God has deserted you, be assured that God is not as distant as you think. Just ask Jonah. "Then Jonah prayed to the LORD his God from inside the fish. He said, 'I cried out to the LORD in my great trouble, and he answered me. I called to you from the land of the dead, and LORD, you heard me!'" (Jonah 2:1–2 NLT).

Do you think Jonah thought things over for three days before praying? No, I believe as he slid down the fish's esophagus and landed in that cesspool of seaweed and slime, he was fervently praying, confessing his sins, and recommitting his life to serve God. Jonah was doing some real praying.

How and when do we do our best praying? Years ago, Sam Walter Foss wrote a poem called "The Prayer of Cyrus Brown."

> "The proper way for a man to pray,"
> Said Deacon Lemuel Keyes,
> "And the only proper attitude
> Is down upon his knees."

"No, I should say the way to pray,"
Said Reverend Doctor Wise,
"Is standing straight with outstretched arms
And rapt and upturned eyes."

"Oh, no, no, no," said Elder Slow,
"Such posture is too proud.
A man should pray with eyes fast-closed
And head contritely bowed."

"It seems to me his hands should be
Austerely clasped in front
With both thumbs pointing toward the ground,"
Said Reverend Doctor Blunt.

"Last year I fell in Hidgekin's well
Headfirst," said Cyrus Brown,
"With both my heels a-stickin' up
And my head a-pointing down.'

"And I made a prayer right then and there,
The best prayer I ever said,
The prayingest prayer I ever prayed,
A-standin' on my head."[50]

When we're in trouble, when life is falling apart, when our life is threatened, we get right down to the business of praying. This was the prayingest prayer Jonah ever prayed.

---

50. Sam Walter Foss quoted in Ray C. Stedman, *Talking to My Father* (Portland: Multnomah Press, 1975), 27.

Foxhole Praying. Have you ever prayed a "foxhole prayer"? Named after the prayer of a soldier hunkered down in a foxhole while bullets are flying overhead, it is a prayer of panic in a life-threatening situation. The airline is going down. The tornado is moving your way. A diagnosis of a terminal illness. A rattlesnake has bitten you. The boat is taking on water. This is when we pray, "God, if you get me out of this, I'll love you and serve you all my days." Is this a promise most people quickly forget? Sometimes. Is a foxhole prayer a bad thing? The truth is that many of us would never turn to God without going through a crisis, a heartache, or a deep trial. This prayer of Jonah is a foxhole prayer: "I cried out to the LORD in my great trouble, and he answered me. I called to you from the land of the dead, and LORD, you heard me!" (Jonah 2:2 NLT). Jonah prayed it, God heard it, and Jonah meant it.

Did Jonah die and come back to life? Jonah states in verse 2, "From the depths of the grave I called for help, and you listened to my cry." The word "grave" is the Hebrew word *sheol*, the abode of the dead awaiting the resurrection and judgment. Some believe Jonah died, his prayer was an out-of-the-body confession, and then he came back to life. However, *sheol* may also refer to a near-death experience. For example, David talks of a near-death experience using the word "grave" or sheol: "You brought me up from the grave, O LORD. You kept me from falling into the pit of death" (Ps. 30:3 NLT). David didn't die. He was only close to death.

It may be that Jonah was only at death's door and didn't physically die. Or he may have died and been brought back to life. If the latter is true, Jesus' comparison of his death and resurrection to the experience of Jonah takes on deeper meaning.

2. God knows what you're going through.

When you're in crisis, it's normal to wonder if God has written you off. You may ask yourself, *Does God remember me? Does he care about me? If he cares, why doesn't he show up and rescue me?* Jonah discovered God knew what he was going through.

> You threw me into the ocean depths, and I sank down to the heart of the sea. The mighty waters engulfed me; I was buried beneath your wild and stormy waves. Then I said, 'O Lord, you have driven me from your presence. Yet I will look once more toward your holy Temple.' I sank beneath the waves, and the waters closed over me. Seaweed wrapped itself around my head. I sank down to the very roots of the mountains. I was imprisoned in the earth, whose gates lock shut forever. But you, O Lord my God, snatched me from the jaws of death! (Jonah 2:3–6 NLT)

While Jonah was cast into the sea by the sailors (1:15), he acknowledges God as the One who cast him into the deep (2:3). Being thrown into a raging ocean with no land in sight was certain death. The waves smashed over him and tossed him about like an empty bottle (v. 3). This was clearly a near-drowning experience.

The possibility of drowning became very vivid to me when a close friend nearly drowned. While in college, several of us were having a contest to see who could swim the most laps in the pool without taking a breath. One of my friends swam two complete laps, surpassing all of us, and started on his third. I watched as his head surfaced slightly, and then he went back under. He was motionless. I realized he was unconscious and in danger of drowning. Panicked, I jumped in and swam to him, pulled him to the side, and forced the water from his lungs. He quickly revived. No more "holding my breath" swim contests for me.

Jonah was fighting to breathe. The *New Century Version* translates verse 5 this way: "The waters of the sea closed around my throat. The deep sea was all around me; seaweed was wrapped around my head." The phrase "around my throat" is the Hebrew word for "soul," but it can also mean "breath" or "throat." The same word is used twice in Genesis 2:7: "God *breathed* (the life-giving soul-breath) into his nostrils the breath of life, and the man became a *living being* (a living, breathing soul)" (Gen. 2:7, emphasis and explanation supplied). Jonah was fighting for his soul—literally his soul-breath that kept him alive. Water was up around his throat, and he was gasping for breath. Adding to Jonah's distress, the slimy cords of seaweed (which may reach twenty-five feet in length) were wrapped around his head. Yuk!

The inability to breathe is one of the most threatening feelings imaginable. In *The Perfect Storm: A True Story of Men Against the Sea*, Sebastian Junger writes regarding a near-drowning experience.

> The instinct not to breathe underwater is so strong that it overcomes the agony of running out of air. No matter how desperate the drowning person is, he doesn't inhale until he's on the verge of losing consciousness. At that point, there's so much carbon dioxide in the blood, and so little oxygen, that chemical sensors in the brain trigger an involuntary breath whether he's underwater or not. That is called the "break point;" laboratory experiments have shown the break point to come after eighty-seven seconds.[51]

Jonah was drifting in and out of consciousness. This was a surreal experience. While gasping for air and wrapped in seaweed, Jonah likely saw his life flash before his eyes as he cried out in

---

51. Sebastian Junger, *The Perfect Storm: A True Story of Men Against the Sea* (New York: W. W. Norton & Co., 2009), accessed Mar. 31, 2019, www.sebastianjunger.com/the-perfect-storm.

distress. Jonah said, "I have been banished from your sight; yet I will look again toward your holy temple" (v. 4). The temple in verse 4 is the Jerusalem temple while the temple in verse 7 is the dwelling place of God. These two statements—banished from God and looking again to the Jerusalem temple—seem contradictory.

What's going on in his mind? A person fighting for their life will experience a wild assortment of thoughts: *This is what it's like to drown? ... This is how my life ends?* At the same time, they may have thoughts like, *I can't die, my daughter is getting married next month,* or *I have tickets to the game next week.* Individuals near death may picture people at their funeral shaking their heads over a tragic, senseless death. Feelings of shame over wrongs they have done often flood their mind.

One of Harry Truman's favorite stories was about a fellow who suffered a severe blow to the head and was knocked unconscious. Thinking he was dead, his family called the funeral home, who picked him up and placed him in a casket to await burial. The next morning, he sat straight up, blinked, and looked around, trying to sort out the situation: "If I'm alive, what in the world am I doing in this soft, satin-filled box? And if I'm dead, why do I have to go to the bathroom"?[52] For Jonah, this fish stomach was like a coffin, and he may not have known if he was dead or alive.

Jonah was rescued from the clutches of death. In Jonah's mind, the belly of this fish was his grave. "I descended to the roots of the mountains. The earth with its bars was around me forever" (2:6). City gates were locked with giant sized bars. Jonah realizes that the earth beneath barred him in forever—in other

---

52. Harry Truman cited by Charles Swindoll, "Disorientation," *Insights* (Fullerton, CA: Insight for Living), 14.

words, the bars were the locks to the underworld, and the bars of death had enclosed him forever.[53] God snatched him from the clutches of near death, or it is possible, he died, and God brought him back to life.

3. God loves you more than you know when you're in the pit (or the pits).

I love the humorous title Erma Bombeck gave to her book: *If Life is a Bowl of Cherries, What Am I Doing in the Pits?* We all go through experiences when life is a pit or the pits. We ask ourselves, *Is God finished with me?*

Jonah must have wondered this, but now he reflects on God's love for him when he was in the pit. The pit had a purpose.

> I sank down to the very roots of the mountains. I was imprisoned in the earth, whose gates lock shut forever. But you, O LORD my God, snatched me from the jaws of death! As my life was slipping away, I remembered the LORD. And my earnest prayer went out to you in your holy Temple. Those who worship false gods turn their backs on all God's mercies. But I will offer sacrifices to you with songs of praise, and I will fulfill all my vows. For my salvation comes from the LORD alone."
>
> Then the LORD ordered the fish to spit Jonah out onto the beach. (Jonah 2:6–10 NLT)

WHAT DID JONAH LEARN IN REHAB?

There are at least two purposes for what God was teaching the prophet during his time in rehab—or, as he calls it in verse 6, "the pit."

---

53. John R. Kohlenberger III, *Jonah and Nahum* (Chicago: Moody Press, 1984), 52.

First, Jonah discovered God was shouting "I love you."

Is there any other reason for God to spare the life of an openly rebellious, spiritually calloused, prejudiced, paranoid, bigoted, selfish, stubborn prophet? Why would God go to the trouble of whipping up a storm, arranging for sailors to throw him overboard, appointing a fish to swallow him, and seeing that he was spit out before he died? Was God desperate because of a shortage of prophets so he had to get Jonah straightened out? God didn't need Jonah. Jonah needed God. Though he had a hard time hearing him in the noise and confusion inside that fish, God was shouting, "Jonah, I love you."

Just ask King David about God's love when he was in the pits. "He lifted me out of the pit of despair, out of the mud and the mire. He set my feet on solid ground and steadied me as I walked along. He has given me a new song to sing, a hymn of praise to our God. Many will see what he has done and be amazed. They will put their trust in the LORD" (Ps. 40:2–3 NLT).

Jeremiah was thrown into a literal pit and thought his life was over. "They threw me into a pit and dropped stones on me. The water rose over my head, and I cried out, 'This is the end!' But I called on your name, LORD, from deep within the pit. You heard me when I cried, 'Listen to my pleading! Hear my cry for help!' Yes, you came when I called; you told me, 'Do not fear'" (Lam. 3:53–57 NLT).

Jonah realizes at the bottom of the sea that God is immersing him in amazing grace. He overflows with a song of thanksgiving—the song from the heart of a person who is loved and shown undeserving grace.

Why does God rescue you and me from the pit? God is shouting, "I love you. I love you so much I am sparing your life. I love you with undeserving grace. My love is getting you ready for a bright future. I love you. Period."

Second, Jonah was learning to surrender his will to God.

Twice Jonah uses the phrase "I will"—*I will* offer sacrifices to you with songs of praise, … *I will* fulfill all my vows (Jonah 2:9 NLT, emphasis supplied). Jonah was now willing to yield his will to the will of God. A turning point. Learning to surrender the will to God is often a process. Step one for Jonah was "go to Nineveh and preach." After his rehab experience, he obeyed. Step two was "love the people of Nineveh." I would like to think Jonah yielded his will and grew to love the people of Nineveh; however, we don't know that he completed this step.

Rehab is always about the will, perhaps because we're weak-willed or strong-willed or a combination of both. We discover too late in life that training the "I will" is more important than training the "I.Q." Unfortunately, most formal training is focused on the intellect rather than the will. We're all born with a strong-willed, stubborn streak. And at the same time, we're afflicted with a weak will. Few yield their will quickly to God. For most of us, submission requires a process of broken plans, shattered dreams, and personal tragedies before we yield. When does a compulsive spender learn to stop spending and cool the credit cards? After the car, TV, or sometimes the house is repossessed? When does a reckless driver learn seat belts and speed limits are for their safety? After a tragic accident? When does a belittling, critical husband or wife come to their senses regarding their destructive habit? After losing the one they love? What does it take to wake up the arrogant who refuse to say, "I am sorry, I was wrong! Will you forgive me?" Shattered relationships? Failed plans? These are the tools God uses to bring us to surrender.

WHY WE ALL NEED REHAB

We think of rehab for alcoholics, gamblers, and druggies. But we all need rehab. Each of us has a heart problem: "The heart is more deceitful than all else and is desperately sick; who can understand it?" (Jer. 17:9). God says the deceit in our heart is a sickness. We're born with a deceitful streak. In most cases, we lie to ourselves more than we lie to others. We pretend that everything is fine when we're falling apart. We fake loving someone while in our heart, we can't stand them. We say things like, "I don't need God running my life." "I'm capable of handling things myself." "I'm not as bad a sinner as that other person." "No one will know if I cheat a little." Rehab is facing the truth about yourself, others, and God. Because of his great love for us, God leads us through rehab.

Jonah exclaims, "Salvation is from the LORD" (v. 9). The word salvation is related to the word "salvage," "to restore," "to rehabilitate." If you've never invited Christ into your life, see Appendix A to learn more about this invitation. This is the most wonderful gift you'll ever receive.

Salvation occurs at the moment of our conversion and new birth, but salvation is also an ongoing process. As Paul said, "Keep on working to complete your salvation with fear and trembling, because God is working in you to help you want to do and be able to do what pleases him" (Phil. 2:12–13 NCV). Work out what God has done within. This is "in-n-out" theology—practice what you believe. This does not mean that we earn salvation by works, but instead, Paul is saying we need to actively allow the Lord to take full control of our outward life. Oswald Chambers said, "You did not do anything to achieve your salvation, but you must do something to exhibit it. ... If you are still the same miserable, grouchy person, set on having your own way, then it is a lie to say that God has saved and sanctified you."[54]

Rehab or brokenness is God's loving process to shape us until the love of God shines through. God initiates rehab through a wide variety of ways: broken dreams, loss of work, business failure, divorce, anger, addictive behavior, isolation and loneliness, sickness, depression to name a few. These situations—as painful as they are—are what God uses to refine us. There are two primary rehab areas where all of us need help.

REPAIRING RELATIONAL BROKENNESS

Relationships rub. Why? If you're in the middle of a muddled conflict that keeps you awake at night and gives you indigestion during the day, you have certainly wondered why. In many—but not all—these situations, rehab is in process. God is at work.

Most of us think of ourselves as a loving person, but when we're truthful to the core, we must admit there are some people we can't stand. We dislike them so fiercely, the thought of showing love to them is on our "never, no way" list. We feel about them the way Jonah felt about Ninevites. This is the "I Love the World—It's People I Can't Stand" dichotomy. There is a disconnect between intentionality and behavior. While, in most of your relationships, you are a very loving person, there may be a few rascals you can't stand. They've shafted you, betrayed you, lied to you, trampled on you, … the list goes on. If you find yourself refusing to forgive, pack your bags and get ready to check in to rehab. Until you're ready to say along with Jesus, "Father, forgive them, for they don't know what they are doing"

---

54. Oswald Chambers, "May 15," in *My Utmost for His Highest* (Grand Rapids, MI: Discovery House Publishers, 1935).

(Luke 23:34 NLT), you need rehab and brokenness. However, struggling to forgive is quite different than refusing to forgive.

Relational storms—and we all have them from time to time—are pretty good indicators that God is working on us. When a relationship goes haywire, rather than blaming the other person, it's a good opportunity to examine your own life. Ask yourself, *What is in me, Lord, that needs changing? Am I prideful, demanding my own way? What are my blind spots?* Augustine said, "O Lord, deliver me from this lust of always vindicating myself."[55] It's the art of excusing ourselves by blaming the other person—something we inherited from our great grandparents, Adam and Eve. Conflicts may arise that have nothing to do with these issues but check your heart and behaviors to see what may need changing.

TAMING THE WILD STALLION OF THE SOUL

When I was six or seven years old, I visited the ranch of family friends. They were in the process of breaking a horse. They lifted me on the horse, and not knowing better, I kicked its flank (the area where the hind legs meet the internal organs just behind the rib cage). The horse reared up and threw me off. My head hit the ground, I suffered a severe concussion and awoke three days later. Since then, I've been very cautious about getting on a horse, though I still ride on occasion.

Horses are amazing creatures designed by God. By their nature, they are wild. Without being broken, a horse doesn't like having someone putting a bit in their mouth or riding on their back. Alan Nelson, using this illustration, describes the first day a wild stallion had someone on his back. "… he (the cowboy) placed one boot in the left stirrup and swung his right foot over the tall horse. For the first time the stallion carried a rider. The

55. Chambers, "Nov. 23," in *My Utmost for His Highest.*

horse turned ninety degrees and began running and kicking to the far end of the corral … He bucked and snorted and bellowed. The twisting jumps threw the cowboy off balance … Two bucks later, the cowboy tumbled to the churning dirt below.[56]

After calming the horse down, he repeated the process several times. Within an hour the cowboy was riding this formerly wild stallion.

The process of breaking a horse is a good thing—essential for the usefulness of this powerful creature. Breaking the horse is far different than beating the horse. Similarly, God works, not to destroy us, but to break us for usefulness. Brokenness is a good thing.

A poster in my granddaughter Siobhan's room says, "We're all broken. That's what lets God's light shine through." Conversely, at the points where we're not broken and yielded, the love and character of God are blocked.

LEARNING THE POWER OF BEING POWERLESS

My wife, Joanne, is a godly person—forgiving, never malicious, filled with love and compassion for people. She was raised by godly parents. She's never needed rehab for drugs or alcohol—she's never used any addictive substance. But Joanne needed rehab.

I grew up in an angry, dysfunctional home. I came into our marriage with buried anger and depression. I couldn't handle criticism. When Joanne married me, I came packaged with all my issues. Joanne was a psychiatric nurse who married a great little fixer-upper. I needed rehab. While I was coming to terms with my broken relationship with my father, Joanne was coming to terms with manipulating and attempting to control the chaos

---

56. Alan E. Nelson, *Broken in the Right Place* (Nashville: Thomas Nelson Publishers, 1994), 4.

caused by my buried anger and depression. She spent Saturday mornings for many months working through Scripture dealing with the Twelve Steps and releasing her need to be controlling. She says, "When I release control and surrender to God, things go much better, and I am at peace."

The Twelve Steps have been a help for millions of people. There are several Scripture-focused Twelve-Step groups including Celebrate Recovery, Overcomers Outreach, and Recovery in Christ Ministries. These groups offer a solid, biblical approach to the Twelve Steps. John Baker started Celebrate Recovery in 1990 as a ministry of Saddleback Church, and now the program is being used in 35,000 churches nationwide with over five million people participating. Celebrate Recovery was introduced at the Southern New Mexico Correction Facility in Las Cruces, New Mexico with amazing results. Today, many prisons and jails in the United States and other countries use Celebrate Recovery.

While God is clearly the "higher power" in Celebrate Recovery and other Christian groups, Christians often object to the "believing in your higher power" in the Twelve Steps of Alcoholics Anonymous (and other similar anonymous groups for gamblers, drug users, codependents, overeaters, and more). In AA, your higher power can be the universe, the stars or moon, the ocean, mother nature, or your speed boat. As a result, many Christians have written off AA and other anonymous groups because of this vague reference to a higher power rather than God. I wholeheartedly agree with this concern, but rather than reject the Twelve Steps totally, I take a different approach. Believing in a vague higher power is not salvation, but it can prepare someone for discovering a personal relationship with God.

I LOVE THE WORLD—IT'S PEOPLE I CAN'T STAND

A few years back, Joanne and I attended a timeshare presentation in Palm Springs with the incentive of a couple nights of free lodging. The sales rep greeted us and invited us to join him in the golf cart for the tour. I quickly noticed his extreme facial redness and spider veins—often an indicator of years of alcoholism. He asked what we did professionally. Joanne said, "I'm a registered nurse," and I replied, "I am a pastor."

Hearing this, he leaned forward with intensity, "Can I talk with you and ask you some questions?" I said, "Certainly, you have me for the next two hours!" He said his wife left him after years of abusing alcohol, but now he was a recovering alcoholic and faithfully going to AA meetings.

His first question, "Who or what is the higher power?" For the next two hours, I explained who Jesus is—the true higher power. He was fascinated, and we didn't really talk about buying a timeshare (which was fine by me). At the close, he said, "You probably don't want to buy a timeshare, but I am so grateful you explained to me who Jesus is. I want him to be my higher power." We prayed with him and welcomed him into the family of God. AA brought him to the threshold of believing in God and prepared him to acknowledge Christ as his higher power.

The Twelve Steps are filled with biblical principles and truth. It's no wonder they are so effective in helping set people free from what sets them back. Practicing the Twelve Steps has been helpful for me. I've had to face my issue: I'm a glutenous overeater. Some folks are into a gluten-free diet ... I'm still working on a gluttony-free diet. I admire those who can eat two cookies. I'm more likely to eat a dozen cookies and fall into a sugar-addicted pattern. This is addictive behavior. I rewrote the Twelve Steps in the first person to apply them to my food addiction.

1. I admit I am powerless over food—which makes my life unmanageable.

2. I believe that God's power is greater than myself and can restore me to sanity.

3. I made a decision to turn my will and my life over to the care of God.

4. I made a searching and fearless moral inventory of myself.

5. I admitted to God, to myself, and another human being the exact nature of my wrongs.

6. I am entirely ready to have God remove all these defects of character.

7. I humbly ask God to remove my shortcomings.

8. I made a list of all the people I harmed and became willing to make amends to them all.

9. I made direct amends to such people wherever possible, except when to do so would injure them or others.

10. I continue to take a personal inventory of my life, and when I am wrong, I promptly admit it.

11. I diligently seek through prayer and meditation and scripture reading to improve my relationship with God, praying only for his will for me and his power to carry that out.

12. I am experiencing a spiritual awakening, and I look for opportunities to carry this message to others and practice these principles in all my affairs.

You can use the Twelve Steps above for any area of struggle in your life, looking to Jesus as your higher power. If you need help identifying your area of need, the list below will help. Insert your sin bent into the Twelve Steps above and begin the process.

COMMON SIN BENTS

Abusing others

Abusing yourself

Addictive behavior

Blaming, fault-finding

Complaining, whining

Conceited, self-important

Conniving, devious

Controlling, nagging

Critical, cutting

Deceitful, fraudulent

Demanding

Divisive, contentious

Drunkenness

Gluttony

Gossipy, nosy

Greedy, stingy

Independent spirit

Jealousy, envy

Lustful, immoral

Manipulating, using others

Materialism, idolatry

Needing to always be right

Occult activity

Pornography

Quarelling, disputing

Rebellious

Rude, insensitive

Resentful, bitter

Selfish ambition

Sexual immorality

Substance abuse

Swearing, profanity

Uncontrolled temper

Violent behavior

LIVE **SMART**
Surrendered **M**ental **A**ttitude **R**egarding **T**ransformation

When I overeat, I hurt myself. Not taking care of myself is dumb. To help me think differently, I've adapted a motto for my life: *Live SMART*. I use this acronym as a daily reminder.

Surrender is the act of yielding my will to God. When I do this, I have a different mindset and attitude. However, my old self can still put up quite a fight. When I yield to it, things get messy in a hurry. When I start thinking I can change myself, I set myself up for disappointment. This is when I need the reminder to *Stop Striving and Live SMART.* Striving is the direct opposite of surrender. God, not me, is doing the transforming. All I can do is surrender to him throughout each day and *Live SMART.*

In my earlier book *Your Winning Edge: God's Power Perfected in Weakness,* I wrote:

> Without brokenness, it's easy to drift along—self-sufficient, seemingly strong, judgmental and self-righteous, demanding of others and often blaming them, expecting to be served rather than serving, unmoved by the pain of others, and an all-around nuisance to live with. With crushing and breaking, you become keenly aware of your weaknesses, valuing others over yourself, and yielding rights. You respond to others with graciousness, humbled by how much you have to learn. You become willing to forgive others with the awareness of your need for forgiveness, developing compassion for others when they hurt. Your faith deepens and matures.[57]

One of my pastor friends told me that a fairly large percentage of his congregation had gone through recovery. His observation: "There is a big difference between those who have gone through recovery and those who have not. Those who have gone through the Twelve Steps are a delight to work with—humble in spirit, teachable, kind, and gracious. They have learned brokenness."

---

57. Beckwith, *Your Winning Edge: God's Power Perfected in Weakness* (Plymouth, MA: Elk Lake Publishing, Inc, 2009) 28.

On the other hand, those who have not gone through recovery are much more difficult to work with. Too many of them are arrogant, stubborn, and disagreeable." This reinforces the truth: we all need rehab.

Nancy DeMoss, writing in an excellent book entitled *Brokenness: The Heart God Revives,* stated it this way, "He (God) wants to restore our 'first love' for Jesus, rekindle the fire of devotion that once burned brightly in our hearts, reconcile broken relationships, and rebuild the parts of our lives that are in a state of disrepair. In short, He wants to revive our hearts. *And it all begins with brokenness and humility.* No exceptions. No shortcuts. No substitutes."[58]

The first step in the Twelve Steps is a simple acknowledgment: *I admit I am powerless over ...* If you've ever said, "I wish I could stop doing ...," this principle is what you've been looking for. This is usually preceded by a long pattern of trying and failing.

We're still kicking and bucking. We think we can do it. We try harder. We pretend everything is fine while we continue to flounder and fail.

When we realize we're broken, powerless, down for the count, helpless, we're ready for step two: *I believe that God's power is greater than myself and can restore me to sanity.* God's power takes over at the point of our surrender and brokenness.

---

58. Nancy Leigh DeMoss, *Brokenness: The Heart God Revives* (Chicago: Moody Press, 2005), 21.

REHAB IN A DARK CANYON

My first seven years as a pastor were exciting on the one hand but rocky and tumultuous on the other. In my fourth year, I was thrust into a situation that was far above my ability to cope. I decided I wanted out.

PASTORAL PAIN

From 1970 to 1975, I worked with John Wimber at Yorba Linda Friends Church in Yorba Linda, California. Before coming to Christ at age twenty-nine, John was the keyboardist, vocalist, and manager for the Paramours Group, later known as the Righteous Brothers. In 1963, John became a Christian and in 1970 was selected as one of the pastors at Yorba Linda Friends Church. In my first pastoral position following my theological training, I worked under John and learned a great deal from him.

John Wimber left the staff of Yorba Linda Friends Church in 1975 to work with the Fuller School of Church Growth. In 1977, with the church sharply divided over charismatic and cultural issues, the board fired a much-loved senior pastor. As executive pastor, they asked me to take the lead. On April 27, 1977, John and I met for four hours at Fuller Seminary, and I suggested we launch a new work. John would lead the departing congregation, and I would lead the remaining group. We further agreed there would be no recruiting between the two groups—individuals would be free to make their own choice to stay or leave. This was the birth of what later became the Vineyard Movement. About half the church left with John, and initially, they became Calvary Chapel Yorba Linda. However, Chuck Smith and the Calvary Chapel leadership had differences with John relating mainly to the practice of spiritual gifts and healing. Wimber and his followers left Calvary Chapel and joined a small group of churches started by Kenn Gulliksen, known as Vineyard Christian Fellowship. With John's leadership, this became the international Vineyard Movement.

Left behind was a wounded congregation bleeding emotionally. Many were angry and hurt over the firing of the previous senior pastor. During this period of upheaval, fear was rampant as to who would leave next. Contrary to what had been agreed on, the departing congregation recruited intensely, and in some cases, husbands and wives chose separate churches, dividing families. I was getting desperate calls at all hours, "So and so is thinking of leaving. They are being recruited. You've got to get over there and rescue them." My associate pastor, Gary Tangeman, became a soulmate assisting me as we confronted one difficult situation after another.

As a twenty-nine-year-old senior pastor, I was in over my head. A few good things were happening in the church—new families joining the church and some numerical growth. However, I was so buried in the pain, I was oblivious to the positive. The tension and strain began to tear me apart. I was having great difficulties sleeping and became severely depressed. I was unable to verbalize what I was feeling—even to Joanne—which made things worse. Relationships at the board level were caustic rather than supportive. Naively, I thought a wounded congregation would pull together with compassion and concern for each other.

On the contrary, the woundedness showed in emotionally charged meetings, angry confrontations, constant blaming, and petty jealousies. I found it impossible to deal with all the expectations thrust on me. Slowly, I was feeling crushed under the weight of conflicting expectations and anger. I wanted out!

In January of 1980, I left to serve as Program Director for Mt. Gilead Bible Conference Center in Northern California.

I also served as pastor for a small church of lumberjacks in the backwoods, Cazadero Community Church, while doing camp ministry. This was a safe haven without the pressures of the senior pastor role. I still loved God and wanted to serve him, but I told God I never wanted to be a senior pastor again. God knew I needed a change, but my refusal to lead a church as a senior pastor was a form of running from God. From time to time, invitations would come to serve as a senior pastor of a multi-staff church, and I would bristle with resistance.

LESSONS LEARNED FROM A 40-FOOT FALL

In July of 1982, I accepted the invitation to speak for a week at Triumphant Life Camp in Bridgeville, about forty-five miles from Eureka, California. During the winter of that year, heavy winter rains had caused flooding and landslides. The embankment of the mountain stream, Butte Creek, that flowed into the Little Van Duzen River near the camp had collapsed into the canyon below leaving shrubbery and tree branches hanging over the edge. The ground appeared to extend as far as the shrubbery and tree branches when in fact, they camouflaged a forty-foot drop.

The summer day had been scorching. I spoke for the first session, and then went for a walk. About a half mile from the camp, I flipped my flashlight off, looked up at the stars, breathed deeply of the fresh mountain air, took a couple of steps, and suddenly I was airborne … free falling with no idea of what was below! In my lighter moments, I joke that the flight was fine, but the landing was rough. The truth is the flight was terrifying, and the landing was bone cracking. When I landed in the bottom of the creek bed, I felt shock waves go up my spinal column. I knew my spine was injured. With pain screaming through my body, I prayed, "Oh, God, you spared my life. I give myself to you for whatever you want." With my back fractured in three places and a broken left shoulder, I screamed for help, but no one heard me. No cell phone in those days. As camp speaker, I had my own cabin, so no one knew I was gone from the camp, and I wondered how I would ever be found. I was at my lowest … and God showed me his love in a remarkable way.

In the depth of that canyon, school was in session. God was teaching me, breaking me, shaping me, and humbling me. What was God telling me in my despair?

First, I AM with you and love you … even in this dark canyon.

I felt terribly alone and frightened. But God was with me, and he heard me. "Even when I walk through the darkest valley (the valley of the shadow of death), I will not be afraid, for you are close beside me" (Ps. 23:4 NLT). Most people do not survive a forty-foot fall, and those who survive are usually paralyzed for life.

In my pain and embarrassment (how could I be so stupid to walk off a cliff?), I felt the calm assurance of God's love. The words of Paul came to mind. "For I am convinced that neither death, nor life, nor angels, nor principalities, nor things present, nor things to come, nor powers, nor height, nor depth, nor any other created thing, will be able to separate us from the love of God, which is in Christ Jesus our Lord" (Rom. 8:38–39).

Second, I AM your strength … even when you are totally weak and utterly helpless.

Looking up at the faint outline of the steep embankment, I told myself—*not a chance—it is impossible to climb that cliff.* In my panic and despair, an amazing number of Scriptures flashed through my mind. I recalled the promise of Jesus to Paul, "My power works best in weakness" (2 Cor. 12:9 NLT). Was it true that God's power could empower me in my weakness? After praying for about twenty minutes, I decided to see if I could stand up. The pain screamed through my body as I attempted to get on my feet. I could lift myself by using my unbroken shoulder and arm on the ground, but I couldn't get all the way up. I slumped back to the ground. In desperation, I prayed for strength. Again, I attempted to stand up. The pain was excruciating as I struggled to lift myself a few inches at a time. Finally, though stooped over, I was standing!

Next, I tried to take a few steps. Little by little, I hobbled with a slow, painful shuffle proceeding upstream in the rocky terrain. Would there be a place to get out of the canyon? I didn't know, but this was my best hunch. After several hours of limping along, I noticed the cliff descending to about four feet high. With pain shooting through my body, I forced myself to roll up on the embankment. I lay there for a few minutes before going through the painful process of standing up. It was about midnight now, and I had left the camp around 8 p.m. I reversed course and began the long journey toward the camp. At one point, I came to a barbed wire fence. There was no way I could part the wires to crawl through the fence, so I laid flat on the ground, held the barbed wire up, and moved my body inch by inch to get under the fence. The pain was so intense I wasn't sure I would make it. After moving a few inches, I would lie still before attempting the next move. Once on my feet again, I continued to shuffle along until I arrived in the camp about 1:30 a.m. A married couple who were camp counselors that week spotted me: "That's the speaker for camp this week. He looks as if he is injured." They came running over and lifted me into the passenger seat of their pickup and drove me to Redwood Memorial Hospital in Fortuna, about an hour away. Once inside the vehicle, my body stiffened so I could barely move. At the hospital, I couldn't get out of the vehicle on my own power, so medical personnel lifted me out and put me on a gurney. It was now about 2:30 a.m. Through all this, what was God teaching me?

Third, I AM teaching you surrender ... instead of striving.

I was a stubborn, struggling person thinking my will could accomplish most anything—that is, if my resolve were strong enough. I wrote New Year's resolutions every year, and they lasted ... at least to the end of the Rose Bowl game. If my resolve had worked, I would have been an amazing person, self-powered to perfection. After my resolutions failed, I would flounder and indulge my self-centered desires before writing another set of resolutions. For example, when my goal was to control my eating, and I failed, I would go on a food binge. I always felt if I could write the perfect goals and dial my will up to the strongest level, I would succeed. As a result, I lived with continual frustration and self-berating because I couldn't keep my resolutions. My life was a yo-yo of self-disappointment.

In the depth of that canyon, God was beginning the process of breaking my will. After the fall, I realized—*striving is entirely different than surrender.* Both involve my will and an action of my will. For me, striving assumed the power of my will to achieve and conquer. The surrender of my will, the direct opposite, helped me understand the utter weakness of my will power. Striving for me was the yearning pride of my old self wanting to look good. I rationalized: *I am so disciplined, my will achieved it, don't I look great.* I discovered surrender is the humble yielding of my will to his will. What a difference! I no longer make New Year's resolutions on December 31 or any other time of the year.

Instead, I ask God for a New Year's revolution. I identify areas where I need to surrender my will to his control.

Fourth, I AM your healer ... and I spared your life for a reason.

Why didn't my life end in that fall? Why am I not a quadriplegic? I don't understand this fully, but I do know God kept me alive for a reason. After the fall, my left shoulder was broken, and I had three compression fractures in my lower back. During six weeks of lying flat, I had a lot of time to think, pray, and reflect on my calling. God has been my healer—amazingly, I have not had back problems. Shortly after my fall, God directed me to be the senior pastor for a church—a church I had said no to numerous times during the year preceding the fall. In the years that have followed, I see God working out his promise for my life: "The Lord will work out his plans for my life—for your faithful love, O Lord, endures forever" (Ps. 138:8 NLT).

THE BLESSING OF BROKENNESS

What is your stubborn Achilles heel? Where does pride rear its ugly head in your life? What are you trying to control? What controls you? Who's the impossible person you can't stand? Have you experienced the blessing of brokenness? This is your moment to deal with it. Here's how.

Stop ... long enough to realize what you're doing, who is being affected, what the potential consequences may be, and why you're doing what you're doing. Assess the high cost to your health and peace of mind when you hang on to bitterness.

Yield ... whatever stands between you and God's perfect will. If it is an affair, anger, resentments, material objects, worry, a wounded relationship, a son or daughter, a destructive habit, whatever, yield it to God today. Admit that you are powerless. Say it and mean it, "I am willing to surrender ..."

Make a U-turn ... repent of your ways. Repentance is a 180-degree turn in your life. Renew your commitment to faithfulness. Set a new direction. Writing down your pledge is better than getting choked by seaweed and drowning in the slime of stubbornness ... or falling off a cliff. "The LORD is close to the brokenhearted and saves those who are crushed in spirit" (Ps. 34:18 NLT).

BROKENNESS IS A GOOD THING!

TIME OUT

CHAPTER FOUR

CHECKIN' INTO REHAB

I cried out to the LORD in my great trouble, and he answered me. I called to you from the land of the dead, and LORD, you heard me! You threw me into the ocean depths, and I sank down to the heart of the sea. The mighty waters engulfed me; I was buried beneath your wild and stormy waves. (Jonah 2:2–3 NLT)

GROW AND APPLY

◊ Read Jonah 2:1–10.

◊ David recalls a time when he was in the pits, and God rescued him. "I waited patiently for the LORD; he turned to me and heard my cry. He lifted me out of the slimy pit, out of the mud and mire; he set my feet on a rock and gave me a firm place to stand. He put a new song in my mouth, a hymn of praise to our God. Many will see and fear and put their trust in the LORD" (Ps. 40:1–3 NLT).

◊ When have you felt like you were in a pit of despair? What were your thoughts and fears?

_____

_____

_____

_____

_____

_____

◊ What areas do you need to surrender? Look back at the list of Common Sin Bents and Behaviors in this chapter.

_____

_____

_____

_____

_____

_____

PRAY

◊ Surrender these areas to the Lord. Allow yourself to be brokenhearted as you pray through these verses.

"The LORD is near to the brokenhearted and saves those who are crushed in spirit" (Ps. 34:18).

"The sacrifice you desire is a broken spirit. You will not reject a broken and repentant heart, O God" (Ps. 51:17 NLT).

"He heals the brokenhearted and binds up their wounds" (Ps. 147:3).

SHARE

This week be alert to people you meet who are in despair or brokenhearted. Give them the gift of compassionate listening. Here are a couple of thought-provoking questions to ask when the time is right.

1. What is the most difficult think you have been through?
2. Is there a time when you've been brokenhearted?
3. Did you feel God was far away or near when you were brokenhearted?

TIME TOGETHER

CHAPTER FOUR

CHECKIN' INTO REHAB

If you're leading a small group, teaching a Bible class, or sharing with the family, below are some opening questions. For the content of the lesson, use the Grow and Apply, Prayer, and Share sections with your Time Out.

CONNECT
1. What is the most difficult thing you have been through?

_____

_____

_____

_____

_____

_____

2. Describe how you felt going through this difficult time.

_____

_____

_____

_____

_____

CHAPTER FIVE

THE GREAT AWAKENING

Eric Fellman writes of visiting a state-sponsored church service in China. This was a country church that had been closed for years by the communists but finally allowed to reopen. On this Sunday, 1400 worshippers crammed into the five hundred-seat auditorium for the service. The sermon consisted mostly of party doctrine: "God would have you meet your quotas," and "God would have you be a model citizen." The audience was quiet and subdued. There was no presentation of the gospel or the living hope in Christ.

At the close of the service, an elderly pastor was asked to bring the prayer. A Chinese friend sitting next to Eric mentioned that the pastor had just been released from prison after twenty years for preaching the gospel. Now, they allowed him to function only in a state-sponsored church with government officials in charge.

His prayer opened with a few phrases, and then Eric heard the Chinese word for "Jesus." The effect on the congregation was electric. When they heard the name of Jesus, the worshippers stirred straight in their seats while those standing lifted faces to heaven. The sound of "amen" began to move through the congregation which had been silent throughout the service.

Minute after minute, the pastor's prayer continued. He was praying the message of God's love and forgiveness. As he came to the close of his prayer, the worshippers spontaneously rose to their feet and then with faces beaming they burst into song, "Blessed be the Name."[59] The powerful name of Jesus could not be silenced even in a church tightly controlled by the communist state.

China became a communist country after a long struggle—a civil war that began in 1927 and continued until 1950 with two phases, 1927 to 1937 and 1946 to 1950. On October 1, 1949, Mao Zedong proclaimed the creation of the People's Republic of China, and by December, Chiang Kai-shek and approximately two million Nationalist Chinese retreated from the mainland to the island of Taiwan.[60] Between 1949 and 1952, Maoist fanatics tortured and expelled most of the missionaries from the country. The missionaries who remained were imprisoned and allowed to languish there until their death. Most sources agree that there were about 750,000 Protestant believers in China in 1949.[61]

China had a history of great missionary work. Among the missionary pioneers were J. Hudson Taylor (1832–1905) who founded and led the China Inland Mission with 205 mission stations and over 800 missionaries. With the complete removal of missionaries in 1952, many feared the demise of Christianity. Did Christianity survive?

---

59. Eric Fellman, "At the Name of Jesus," *Moody Monthly* (April 1983), 5.

60. *Wikipedia Encyclopedia,* s.v. "Chinese Civil War," accessed Mar. 31, 2019, www.en.wikipedia.org/wiki/Chinese_Civil_War.

61. Paul Hattaway, "How Many Christians Are in China?" *Asia Harvest,* accessed Mar. 31, 2019, www.asiaharvest.org/how-many-christians-are-in-china-summary/.

In 1958, Mao's wife proudly stated, "Christianity in China has been confined to museums. It is dead and buried."[62] During the Cultural Revolution from 1966 to 1976, all expression of religious life in China was banned. Christians were arrested, imprisoned, and sometimes tortured. Bibles and churches were destroyed, and the Chinese Christians were forced to gather and worship in secret.[63] The house church movement, which began in 1949, exploded during this time. In many respects, the great Cultural Revolution turned into the great Christian Revolution. The persecuted church thrived despite all the attempts to destroy it.

More recently, in 2014, officials broke through human barriers to remove crosses from churches in Wenzhou and Zhejiang provinces, in total destroying about two thousand crosses. In March of 2017, Chinese police in riot gear began breaking into churches in the darkness of night to install surveillance cameras. One camera was pointed at the door to keep track of who entered, a second camera pointed at the pulpit to monitor what was being taught, a third camera was facing the congregation while a fourth camera was pointed at the tithe box. To make matters worse, the churches were required to pay for the cost of the cameras.[64]

---

62. "How Many Christians are in China? *God Does Not Believe in Atheists,* last modified Sept. 17, 2015, accessed Mar. 31, 2019, www.goddoesnotbelieveinatheists.wordpress.com/tag/number-of-christians-in-china/.

63. *New World Encyclopedia,* s.v. "Christianity in China," last modified Feb. 18, 2017, http://www.newworldencyclopedia.org/entry/Christianity_in_China.

64. June Cheng, "Under Big Brother's Eye," *WORLD Magazine,* May 13, 2017, 36–39.

The Golden Lampstand Church, located in Shanxi Province, China, thrived as a megachurch ministering to fifty thousand believers. The communist regime obviously hated this highly effective church, reaching thousands for Christ. On January 12, 2018, they put dynamite to the church and destroyed it. This was the second church destroyed in less than a month. Before and after pictures and further details are available in a *New York Times* article, available at the website in the footnotes.[65] The Communist Party continues to feel threatened by the rapid expansion of Christianity in a nation whose official religion is atheism.

In 1950, there were fewer than a million Protestant Christians in China. How many Christians are in China today? Accurate figures are difficult to determine in a land that is so large and diverse. Estimates range from 100 to 200 million believers. *Asia Harvest* reported 105 million believers in 2011—based on the ten-year study of every province in China by Paul and Joy Hattaway.[66] God alone knows the precise number of believers in China, but without question, Christianity has grown at an astonishing rate.

The explosion of Christianity is embarrassing for China and the Communist party after all their efforts to stomp out Christianity. As a further embarrassment, the number of Christians in China exceeds the membership in the Communist

---

65. Russell Goldman, "Chinese Police Dynamite Megachurch," *New York Times*, Jan. 12, 2018, accessed Mar. 31, 2019, https://www.nytimes.com/2018/01/12/world/asia/china-church-dynamite.html.

66. Paul Hattaway, "How Many Christians are in China?" *Asia Harvest* accessed Mar. 31, 2019, https://asiaharvest.org/how-many-christians-are-in-china-introduction/.

Party which had 88.76 million members in 2016. In fact, China is the largest printer of Bibles in the world. The Amity Printing Company in Nanjing printed 150 million copies between 1987 and 2016 in 90 languages and sold them in 70 countries. There are projections that China may have the largest number of Christians in the world by 2030. [67] *Voice of the Martyrs* reported in 2017, "Worship services are being broken up by baton-wielding police officers, participants arrested, Bibles confiscated, and Christian church buildings demolished. But still, an estimated 3,000 people *every day* come to a knowledge of Jesus Christ in China."[68]

The authorities can remove the missionaries, but they can't remove the Christ that is in the hearts of the people. They can persecute, torture, and imprison Christians, burn Bibles and churches, destroy crosses, but they can't stop the eternal work of God.

Let's look at one of the greatest spiritual movements in all of history found in the book of Jonah, and how you can be part of the spiritual revival and awakening happening today.

HOW TO BE PART OF A GREAT REVIVAL AND AWAKENING

What is the difference between an awakening and a revival? We often hear that our nation needs a great revival. This is true, but our country also needs a great awakening. Revival is

---

67. Sutirtho Patranobis, "Atheist China could have largest number of Christians in the world by 2030," *Hindustan Times*, Dec. 25, 2016, www.hindustantimes.com/world-news/in-atheist-china-christians-outnumber-communist-party-members/story.

68. "3,000 Christians Added Daily in China," *World Net Daily*, last modified Jan. 18, 2017, accessed Mar. 31, 2019, www.wnd.com/2007/01/39732/.

the "rebirth" of something that was once alive. Revival is what Christians and churches need. An awakening is when those without Christ awaken to their need of the Savior and become followers of Jesus. A great revival—repentance and renewal by Christians—often precedes a great awakening—many turning to Christ for the first time. Jonah needed revival, and what follows is the great awakening in Nineveh.

First, surrender completely to God and live with total obedience.

God graciously granted Jonah a second opportunity and directed him to go to Nineveh. "Now the word of the LORD came to Jonah the second time, saying, 'Arise, go to Nineveh the great city and proclaim to it the proclamation which I am going to tell you.' So Jonah arose and went to Nineveh according to the word of the LORD. Now Nineveh was an exceedingly great city, a three days' walk (Jonah 3:1–3).

Isn't God grace and mercy amazing? He gives Jonah a second chance. This is starting over—a fresh run, another opportunity. Where would we be without second, third, or more chances to correct our past mistakes and live for God? We're prone to think because of a past failure, God can no longer use us. This is a lie of Satan. God allows us to start over—he grants second opportunities when we have failed.

Jonah figures out the word *obey* means OBEY! No detours, no arguments, no delays. This time Jonah obeys. Interestingly, Jonah is the only prophet that God sent to a foreign country to deliver his message. Jonah, as we will discover later, is still filled with spite for the people of Nineveh and wants them destroyed. He must have thought to himself, *Ok. I'm going to preach judgment to the despicable people of Nineveh, and God will blast them to smithereens. Serves them right.* Jonah obeys, but he still has the problem of "I Love the World—It's People I Can't Stand." We can legalistically obey God and yet have no tender compassion for people.

If Jonah had been ejected from the fish or whale at Joppa where he boarded the ship, (Jonah 1:3—modern day Jaifa or Haifa), he would have 524 miles to travel to Nineveh. To travel this distance meant that he had to walk about twenty-five or thirty days. Jonah had plenty of time to get worked up about his message of destruction for Nineveh.

Nineveh is described as an "exceedingly great city, a three days' walk" (v. 3), a statement regarding its size as well as its importance. Archaeological excavations indicate that the city of Nineveh was about eight miles around with amazing fortification and a large population. Jonah 4:11 mentions the innocent children as numbering 120,000, which would put the whole population at about a million.[69] Nineveh had a large metropolitan area that was outside the city walls—an area about sixty miles in circumference. "A metropolitan city the size of Nineveh, with a circumference of about 60 mi., would require 3 days just to get around it. These dimensions are confirmed by historians. Stopping to preach would only add to the time requirement.[70]

What does it take to see a great revival and awakening? Examine your life. Is there any questionable practice? Are you obedient to the Lord in every area? Yield and get ready for things to happen.

Ask God to give you a burden for hurting people (including those on your "I can't stand" list). When you're dealing with

---

69. Robert Jamieson, A. R. Fausset, and David Brown, *A Commentary: Critical, Experimental, and Practical on the Old and New Testaments* (Published 1871, database WordSearch: 2012), s.v. "Jonah 3:3."

70. *The MacArthur Study Bible*, 1268.

a mean, nasty person, they are usually that way for a reason. What has life handed them that caused them to become cruel or malicious? God may use you to show them love and bring a great awakening in their life.

Second, proclaim God's message.

At last, Jonah puts his mouth in motion to do as God commanded, "Then Jonah began to go through the city one day's walk; and he cried out and said, 'Yet forty days and Nineveh will be overthrown'" (Jonah 3:4).

Jonah's order was to preach a message of doom to one of the most powerful and perverted cities in the world. Normally, he would expect rejection, hostility, torture, and possibly death. His was a tough, seemingly impossible, assignment. How could he possibly expect these people who were completely hostile to God and hated Jews to repent?

Jesus gave us clear instructions to take the gospel to the ends of the earth. "Go into all the world and preach the gospel to all creation" (Mark 16:15). To get the job done, we're going to have to take the gospel to a lot of people that persecute and hate us— those who may be on our "people I can't stand" list.

Jonah proclaimed a simple eight-word warning of doom and gloom: "Yet forty days and Nineveh will be overthrown" (v. 4). In my opinion, this is the world's worst sermon. No introduction. No outline. No humor to connect with the crowd. No hope for the future. No positive thinking. A totally negative message. The sermon was lousy from my perspective—but at least it was short.

However, the eight words may have been his primary theme—not the sum total of his message. I think Jonah likely shared his personal experience of being rescued from the fish or whale. And Jonah did include an illustration—his personal appearance. What a sight he must have been. The main stomach glands of the whale produce hydrochloric acid and pepsin.[71] If he was in a goliath grouper, the fish's stomach also contains hydrochloric acid at a concentration that will damage the lungs and produce skin burns. Stomach acid, which our body amazingly counteracts, will burn through a piece of wood and destroy metal.[72] The hair on Jonah's body was likely gone, and his skin probably had burned spots along with yellow-brown patches from the hydrochloric acid. Jonah's survival was nothing short of miraculous. He didn't need a loudspeaker or a gospel band to draw attention. Jonah was a circus-like sideshow.

I imagine Jonah stopping at a corner and a crowd gathering. "Hey, buddy, what happened to you?" someone shouts, "You been drinking turtle juice or what?" Jonah picks up on the interest and tells his story. "A fish swallowed me, and I'm alive to tell about it." With the audience riveted at the sight of him, he tells the story of the storm, the sailors, being thrown overboard and swallowed by a fish, the calming of the storm, what it was like inside the fish, and how the fish puked him out. And then Jonah says, "IN FORTY DAYS, NINEVEH WILL BE OVERTURNED! REPENT." I'd repent!

There is another interesting connection in Jonah's message. The word "Nineveh" is derived from the word *Ninua* or *Nina* (i.e., Nimrod who founded Nineveh) meaning "a fish within a

71. "How Does Digestion Take Place in Whales?" *Whales Online,* last modified July 7, 2015, accessed Mar. 31, 2019, www. baleinesen-direct.org/en/how-does-digestion-take-place-in-whales/.

72. "How Powerful is Stomach Acid?" *Wonderopolis,* accessed Mar. 31, 2019, http://wonderopolis.org/wonder/how-power-ful-is-stomach-acid; Paul K. Li, Chris Spittler, Charles W. Taylor, David Sponseller, and Raphael S. Chung, "In Vitro Effects of Simulated Gastric Juice on Swallowed Metal Objects: Implications for Practical Management." *Gastrointestinal Endoscopy 46.2* (1997): 152–55.

house." The *International Standard Bible Encyclopedia* says, "The native name appears as *Ninua* or *Nina* (*Ninaa*), written with the character for 'water enclosure' with that for 'fish' inside. Nineveh was the 'Place of Fish'—great fishing in the Tigris River—indicating the goddess associated with fish and the river. 'Nina' was the fish goddess of the city of 'Nineveh.'"[73] The people also worshiped *Dagon* represented as half man and half fish.[74]

The crowd may have been asking something like this: "You mean you were swallowed by a great fish and your God rescued you. Wow! Your God must be greater than our fish goddess Nina and our fish god Dagon. We're astounded at the power of your God. We believe and repent of our sins."

How does God want you to share his message? I don't recommend marching up and down the street in front of your house dressed in sackcloth shouting, "In forty days, Los Angeles will be overturned! Repent!" There are better ways. Here are four steps to share the gospel.

Step One: Start praying for those in your sphere of influence. Who needs God's love in your circle of relationships? Friends? Extended family? Neighbors? Since we're tackling the "I Love the World—It's People I Can't Stand" issue, start praying for the difficult people in your life. They may be crazy-makers who wield power with the charm of their personality but are destructive in the process.

Step Two: Build a relationship. Get interested in them. Ask caring questions. Find out the concerns in their life. Extend love to them in some practical, need-meeting way.

73. *ISBE,* Vol 4, s.v. "Nineveh."
74. *The MacArthur Study Bible,* 1266.

Step Three: Ask a thought-provoking question. "What's most important to you?" They may say, "My dog ... pizza ... drag racing ... flowers ... my wife or husband ... my children ... my grandchildren." Often, they will say, "Well, I guess God should be most important, but ..." You now have a wide-open door to explain why God is the most important priority in your life. At the end of each chapter in the Time Out, there is a section entitled Share. I have included questions that will help you open dialogue to share your faith using the topic of the chapter. Always seek a friendly dialogue rather than spewing verses or preaching at them.

Step Four: Share the gospel. Warmly, with compassion, gentleness, and respect, tell them how Christ has changed your life. Peter put it this way: "Always *being* ready to make a defense to everyone who asks you to give an account for the hope that is in you, yet with gentleness and reverence;" (1 Pet. 3:15). How do I explain the gospel? I frequently use what I call the **ABC's** backwards: (1) **Confess** your sins; (2) **Believe** in the risen Christ, and (3) **Accept** him into your life to be the resident and president. See Appendix A.

THE GREAT AWAKENING IN NINEVEH

This time Jonah obeyed the LORD's command and went to Nineveh, a city so large that it took three days to see it all. On the day Jonah entered the city, he shouted to the crowds: "Forty days from now Nineveh will be destroyed!" The people of Nineveh believed God's message, and from the greatest to the least, they declared a fast and put on burlap to show their sorrow.

When the king of Nineveh heard what Jonah was saying, he stepped down from his throne and took off his royal robes. He dressed himself in burlap and sat on a heap of ashes. Then the king and his nobles sent this decree throughout the city:

"No one, not even the animals from your herds and flocks, may eat or drink anything at all. People and animals alike must wear garments of mourning, and everyone must pray earnestly to God. They must turn from their evil ways and stop all their violence. Who can tell? Perhaps even yet God will change his mind and hold back his fierce anger from destroying us."

When God saw what they had done and how they had put a stop to their evil ways, he changed his mind and did not carry out the destruction he had threatened. (Jonah 3:5–10 NLT)

Historically, the king of Nineveh was either Shalmaneser IV (782–773 BC) or Assurdan III (772–755 BC). The king of Nineveh was also the king of Assyria. The ruler of the nation would naturally be the ruler of the city, the hub of all the important decisions.[75] The reports of Jonah's bleached face and body and his miraculous experience inside the fish may have preceded him to the palace. The king heard the message and repented—exchanging his royal robes for sackcloth and ashes. Sackcloth, a coarse, dark cloth unfit for normal wear, was a symbol of sorrow and repentance (Rev. 6:12). Utter helplessness and despair were indicated by sitting in ashes (Job 2:8). The entire city joined the king in repenting.

WHAT ABOUT GROUP CONVERSION?

How is it possible for an entire city to repent and turn to God all at the same time? In western culture, this seems highly unlikely if not impossible. We are individualistic. Each person makes their own decision. If a group decides a direction, there are always those who dissent—sometimes just out of stubbornness.

---

75. Gaebelein, *The Expositor's Bible Commentary,* Vol. 7, 382.

I had the privilege of knowing and working with Dr. Clyde Cook as a friend and teacher. Clyde was born in China to missionary parents and served as chairman of the Missions Department at Biola University before becoming president of the university. Clyde often spoke about what is called a "people movement." This is when an entire group of people decides to follow Christ all at the same time. Group conversation sounds strange to us, but when tribes make decisions collectively—where to hunt, who leads the tribe, what customs to follow—it is not unheard of for them to decide as a group to follow Christ.

Mark and Judy Zabel serving with the Malay Baptist Mission went to Borneo. They spent their first year learning the language, building a thatched house, and attempting to make friends with the people.

They were surprised when two elders from a village showed up and asked, "Can you come to our village and tell us more about your God? We want to know more about him."

Mark traveled to the village, and when he arrived, the chief asked him to tell them more about his God. For three hours, Mark talked to the men about the Jesus Way and answered their questions. Following this, the chief asked Mark to sit down on a log, and the men broke up into smaller groups, each made up of men from the same family line. For about thirty minutes, the men debated—arguing for or against following the new God. Finally, the arguments subsided, and the leaders from each lineage gathered with the chief. Another heated debate followed. Finally, the chief announced, "We have all decided to follow the Jesus Way. We want to be baptized."[76]

In a letter to Biola University alumni, Ashley Brady shares the story of a student named Sarah. She was challenged to

---

76. Paul Hiebert, *Case Study: Group Conversion*, accessed Mar. 31, 2019, https://www.home.snu.edu/~hculbert/group.htm.

choose and pray for an unreached people group during a student chapel. She went forward after the chapel and randomly selected the names of two unreached people groups in India called the Jat Sarut and the Jat Virk. For two years, she prayed for these people.

The Lord opened the door for her to go to India with Truthseekers International—a ministry that fights the injustice of the caste system, works for women's rights, and cares for slum children. During the trip, the team traveled to four cities and eight villages sharing the good news of Jesus. Most of the villages were completely unreached and had never seen white people before. Sarah shares her amazing experience.

> The most powerful moment of the trip was when we went to the village of Indragarh. After ministering to the people and ministering in the village, we got a call from the village leaders saying they liked what they heard and the whole village wanted to convert from Hinduism to Christianity. We were blown away that a completely unreached, isolated village made such a huge step towards Christ. … After going to Indragarh, we found out that they were a "Jat" village, the group of people I had been praying for. God had heard my prayers for two years and sent my team to them.[77]

Did Jonah pray for Nineveh? I believe he did. His prayer was probably, "God destroy them with fire and brimstone." Amazingly with such an attitude, things began to happen when Jonah brought the message.

---

77. Ashley Brady, Letter to Biola Alumni, June 5, 2013.

WAS THIS TRUE REPENTANCE?

Genuine repentance has clear markers—indelible indicators of heart change. Here are four reasons we know the Ninevites experienced genuine conversion.

First, they believed God.

"It is impossible to please God without faith. Anyone who wants to come to him must believe that God exists and that he rewards those who sincerely seek him" (Heb. 11:6 NLT).

Belief sank deep into the hearts of the people. God's message spread rapidly through the city, and without exception, met receptive hearts. God may have been at work in advance preparing them for the message of Jonah. If Jonah's mission occurred during the reign of Assurdan III (772–755 BC), we know from history that a famine and plagues may have preceded his arrival as well as an eclipse of the sun in 763 BC. God could have used the severe plagues of 765 and 759 and the total eclipse of 763 B.C. to alert the people to their need. When combined with the work of the Spirit of God, there is sufficient cause for the great repentance recorded.[78]

Second, they repented.

Participation was wide sweeping among the people of the city—all classes of people. Repentance involves mourning—grieving lost opportunity and a broken relationship with God. With repentant hearts, they declared a fast. "Then the people of Nineveh believed in God; and they called a fast and put on

---

78. Walter A. Alcorn, *Book of Jonah*, p. 947, and John H. Walton, *Jonah* (Grand Rapids: Zondervan Publishing, 1981, pp. 40–48, cited by John R. Kohlenberger III, *Jonah and Nahum* (Chicago: Moody Bible Institute, 1984), 60.

sackcloth from the greatest to the least of them. ... both man and beast must be covered with sackcloth; and let men call on God earnestly that each may turn from his wicked way and from the violence which is in his hands" (Jonah 3:5, 8). Even the animals were included. "It was a Persian custom to use animals in mourning ceremonies."[79] When horses pulled the casket in a funeral procession, the horses would be draped with black as a sign of mourning.

Third, they called on God with urgency.

This was a message of extreme urgency, like a warning signal for a national emergency: "let men call on God earnestly that each may turn from his wicked way and from the violence which is in his hands" (v. 8). There was no putting this off for another day. They didn't wait until the thirty-ninth day to repent.

Fourth, they gave up their evil ways and violence.

This was an enormous change, a major overhaul, a clean-up of a corrupt society. As mentioned in chapter one, the city of Nineveh was one of the moral armpits of the world. God spoke of their moral condition like a stench, a foul sick odor: "... I have seen how wicked its people are" (Jonah 1:2 NLT). Implied is a stench of immorality that would rival Sodom and Gomorrah on the all-time filth list. Drunkenness, vice, prostitution, astrology, witchcraft, homosexuality, extreme violence and torture, corruption, ruthless greed. This was Nineveh. These are the deeds Nineveh repented of! The clearest indicator of repentance is turning from sin to follow God.

What turn-around needs to take place in your life? Is there a destructive sin lurking in the shadows? Take the steps the

---

79. *The MacArthur Study Bible*, p. 1268.

Ninevites did: (1) believe God; (2) repent; (3) call on God with urgency; and (4) turn from your sin. God is rich in mercy. God responded to their repentant hearts, and he "relented" (v. 9 and 10) regarding their destruction. God withdrew what they deserved. Never ask God for what you deserve. You don't want that.

An awakening is something that only God can ignite. But you can be a "match in the Masters' hand." Ask God, "Ignite the fire in me."

THE GREAT AWAKENING TODAY

This gospel of the kingdom shall be preached in the whole world as a testimony to all the nations, and then the end will come. (Matt. 24:14)

Behold, a great multitude which no one could count, from every nation and all tribes and peoples and tongues, standing before the throne … (Rev. 7:9)

THE GROWTH OF CHRISTIANITY TODAY

What an incredible day to be alive. God is moving in amazing ways, and the spread of Christianity is surging forward despite horrific persecution—beheadings, beatings, imprisonment, and burning of churches and Bibles.

Paul announced to the skeptics of his day, "Look and perish, you despisers (of the truth), for I am doing something in your day—something that you won't believe when you hear it announced" (Acts 13:41 TLB). What is God doing today?

Let's look at the facts as reported in the *World Christian Encyclopedia* from Oxford University Press, the authoritative, definitive work in the field of international religious demography. It is the most extensive survey of world religions ever attempted.

• Christianity grew from 1.5 billion in 1985 to a little over 2 billion in 2000 (including births and deaths). This was a growth of about 31 million annually or a *daily average of 86,000*. This is the equivalent of adding more than the population of Australia (24.6 million) every year.[80]

• Today, Christianity makes up 32 percent of the world's population. This is not far from the size of the two next largest religions combined—Islam at 23 percent and Hinduism at 15 percent.[81] Christianity is also the only religion represented in all 238 surveyed countries.

The statistics certainly include many who are Christian in name only. God alone knows the number who are turning to him with genuine saving faith. However, the overall numbers are still significant regarding the worldwide impact of Christianity.

I find Christians often disheartened thinking Islam is sweeping the world while Christianity is only holding its own or making little progress. However, in many parts of the Islamic world, there is a great movement of people turning to Christ. The website, *Muslim Statistics*, posted an interview from Arabic TV news. "According to Al-Jazeerah's interview with Sheikh Ahmad Al Katani, the president of The Companions Lighthouse for the Science of Islamic Law in Libya, in every hour, 667 Muslims convert to Christianity. Every day, 16,000 Muslims

---

80. David B. Barrett, *World Christian Encyclopedia* (New York: Oxford University, 1982), 780. Christianity in 1985: 1,548,592,187; in 2000: 2,019,921,366; average annual growth: 31,421,945; average daily growth: 86,088.

81. Pew Research Center Forum on Religion and Public Life, *The Global Religious Landscape*, Dec. 18, 2012, accessed Mar. 31, 2019, https://www.pewforum.org/2012/12/18/global-religious-landscape-exec/

convert to Christianity. Every year, 6 million Muslims convert to Christianity."[82]

It is true that Islam is growing rapidly and may be growing faster than Christianity. Two factors contribute to the rapid growth of Islam: one, Islam is generally located in regions of the world where the birth rate is higher, and Muslims tend to have larger families. Second, many of the converts to Islam are coerced. If someone says, "Become a Muslim, or we'll slit your throat," many will say, "Well, since you put it that way, I guess I'd better become a Muslim." Is this true conversion when people are threatened with a machine gun or a machete?

THE *JESUS* MOVIE

In 1978, my friend Roy Rosedale, a missionary serving with Campus Crusade, handed me a manuscript for a proposed movie based on the life of Christ. He asked that I review the script for biblical accuracy. I carefully read it, made a few notes, and sent it back to him. The script became the *Jesus* movie.

Little did I know the *Jesus* movie would become the most effective evangelistic tool ever developed, viewed by more people than any other movie in history. CRU (formerly Campus Crusade) reports these facts regarding the impact of the *Jesus* movie: "Every eight seconds, somewhere in the world, another person indicates a decision to follow Christ after watching the 'Jesus' film ... that's 10,800 people per day, 324,000 per month and more than 3.8 million per year! That's like the population of the entire city of Pittsburgh, PA coming to Christ every 28 ¼ days. Since 1979 more than 200 million men, women and

82. "Al-Jazeerah: 6 Million Muslims Convert to Christianity in Africa Alone Each Year," *Muslim Statistics*, December 14, 2012, accessed Mar. 31, 2019, muslimstatistics.wordpress.com/2012/12/14/al-jazeerah-6-million-muslims-convert-to-christianity-in-africa-each-year/.

children worldwide have indicated decisions to follow Jesus after viewing the film."[83]

REVIVAL SPREADING LIKE WILD FIRE

Evan Roberts, a simple homespun preacher with little skill as an orator and dust from the coal mines in his hair, had a passion for the Word of God and revival. At age twenty-five, Robert's landlady evicted him for praying and preaching too loudly in his room. He asked his pastor to allow him to preach. Finally, the pastor consented to allow him to speak after the midweek service if anyone chose to stay.

Out of curiosity, seventeen stayed and listened to his simple message: (1) confess every known sin; (2) remove every doubtful practice from your life; (3) obey the Holy Spirit; and (4) go public with your witness for Christ. The next evening, more came to hear him speak and the fire began to spread. In the next thirty days, 37,000 repented of their sins. Within five months, 100,000 were brought into the kingdom of God. The revival moved into England, Western and Northern Europe, Africa, India, China, Korea, and America. Historians estimate that 20 million came to Christ in America.

THE END IS IN SIGHT

What a day of opportunity! Jesus said the end would come when the gospel was proclaimed to the whole world (Matt. 24:14). As the gospel spreads and great awakenings take place in many parts of the world, my heart is filled with anticipation. No one can deny, we're getting closer. Be encouraged. As I write, I

83. "The Jesus Film Project," *Love Alive International*, accessed Mar. 31, 2019, https://lovealiveinternational.com/resources/the-jesus-film-project. For further information, see *Official Jesus Film Project Ministry Statistics-Mar. 1, 2019*; accessed Mar. 31, 2019, https://www.jesusfilm.org/about/learn-more/statistics.html.

can't get the stirring words of the "Battle Hymn of the Republic" out of my mind. Allow the words to grip your heart as well.

> Mine eyes have seen the glory of the coming of the Lord.
>
> He is trampling out the vintage where the grapes of wrath are stored.
>
> He hath loosed the fateful lightning of His terrible swift sword.
>
> His truth is marching on.
>
> Glory, glory, hallelujah! Glory, glory, hallelujah!
>
> Glory, glory, hallelujah! His truth is marching on.

Considering the days we live in, how should we respond? Get right with God—*now*. Abandon every questionable practice. Love Christians. Set down your differences with fellow followers of Christ. Encourage another believer every day. Shake some salt, shine some light. Share your faith. Love the unlovable. Pray for the nations where Christians are being persecuted. Pray, "Come Lord Jesus" (Rev. 22:20).

Dr. James Stewart Edinburgh of Scotland said, "If we can but show the world that being committed to Christ is no tame, humdrum, sheltered monotony but the most thrilling, exciting adventure the human spirit can ever know, those who have been standing outside the church and looking askance at Christ will come crowding to pay allegiance. So, we might well expect the greatest revival since Pentecost."[84]

---

84. Quoted by Dr. Bill Bright, *Crosswalk,* accessed Mar. 31, 2019, https://www.crosswalk.com/devotionals/insights-from-bill-bright/the-most-thrilling-adventure-april-9.html.

TIME OUT

CHAPTER FIVE

THE GREAT AWAKENING

Then the people of Nineveh believed in God; and they called a fast and put on sackcloth from the greatest to the least of them. (Jonah 3:5)

GROW AND APPLY

- Read Jonah 3:1–10.

- The simple message of Evan Robert that sparked a worldwide revival included four steps.
  1. Confess every known sin.
  2. Remove every doubtful practice from your life.
  3. Obey the Holy Spirit.
  4. Go public with your witness for Christ.

- What action does God want you to take?

_____

_____

_____

_____

_____

_____

_____

_____

PRAY

In your time with the Lord, pray through these verses for your life, family, and church.

> Then we will never abandon you again. Revive us so we can call on your name once more (Ps. 80:18 NLT).

> Won't you revive us again, so your people can rejoice in you? (Ps. 85:6 NLT).

> I am exceedingly afflicted; Revive me, O LORD, according to your word (Ps. 119:107).

> For thus says the high and exalted One Who lives forever, whose name is Holy, 'I dwell on a high and holy place and also with the contrite and lowly of spirit in order to revive the spirit of the lowly and to revive the heart of the contrite' (Isa. 57:15).

> Come, let's go back to the LORD. He has hurt us, but he will heal us. He has wounded us, but he will bandage our wounds. In two days he will put new life in us; on the third day he will raise us up so that we may live in his presence and know him. Let's try to learn about the LORD; He will come to us as surely as the dawn comes. He will come to us like rain, like the spring rain that waters the ground (Hos. 6:1–3 NCV).

I LOVE THE WORLD—IT'S PEOPLE I CAN'T STAND

Make a list of those in your sphere of influence—family, friends, neighbors, classmates, fellow employees—and start praying for them.

_____

_____

_____

_____

_____

_____

SHARE

Strike up a conversation with someone today and share your faith. Here are a couple of thought-provoking questions to ask when the time is right.

1. Is our country going forward or backward morally?
2. What does our country need most?

TIME TOGETHER

CHAPTER FIVE

THE GREAT AWAKENING

If you're leading a small group, teaching a Bible class, or sharing with the family, below are some opening questions. For the content of the lesson, use the Grow and Apply, Prayer, and Share sections with your Time Out.

CONNECT
(questions to start the discussion)

◊ How far can a nation decline before God brings judgment?

_____

_____

_____

_____

_____

_____

_____

◊ What would you love to see happen in our community, state, and nation?

_____

_____

_____

_____

_____

_____

CHAPTER SIX

THIS MAKES ME SO MAD

How do you start a war?

Entertain a rumor, jump to a conclusion, get fuming mad, sparks fly, and voilà ... WAR!

"Remember the *Maine*!"[85] was the rage that fueled the Spanish-American War. The American battleship *USS Maine* exploded in the harbor of Havana, Cuba at 9:40 p.m. on February 15, 1898. The ship was stationed there to protect American interests in the war that Cuba was fighting against Spain. Of the 354 on board, 268 lost their lives.

The American press was certain who was responsible for the sinking of the *Maine*. William Randolph Hearst's *New York Journal* published drawings showing how Spanish saboteurs fastened an underwater mine to the *Maine* and detonated it from shore. American citizens were outraged, "How dare they

---

85. "The Destruction of USS Maine," *Naval History and Heritage Command*, 805 Kidder Breese Street, SE, Washington Navy Yard, Washington, D.C. 20374–5060 www.history.navy.mil; Thomas B. Allen, "A Special Report - What Really Sank the MAINE," *National Geographic* (February, 1998); "Remember the Maine," *Small Planet Communications*, 15 Union Street, Lawrence, MA 01840 (978) 794–2201, www.smplanet.com.

sink our ship!" Remember the Maine ignited the fuse, and the United States declared war on Spain.

What really happened? Four examinations of the wreckage have taken place since the ship exploded in Havana Harbor. One was conducted by the United States Court of Inquiry. A second examination was performed by Spanish divers, and a third was performed by the Board of Inspection and Survey. The *Maine* was dewatered by building a cofferdam and every part of the wreckage identified and studied. In 1976, Admiral Hyman G. Rickover published his book, *How the Battleship Maine Was Destroyed*. The fourth study was conducted in 1998 by the *National Geographic* which commissioned the Advanced Marine Enterprises (AME) to prepare a computer model to explore the cause of the *Maine's* destruction. Studies of heat transfer indicated the *Maine's* coal bunker ignited the gunpowder just four inches away behind a quarter-inch-thick steel plate. Not all historians are settled on the subject, but the evidence strongly suggests "the explosion that sank our ship and catapulted us into the Spanish-American War was caused by a blast from twenty thousand pounds of powder ... from the inside."[86]

How many conflicts are fueled by the war cry, "You make me so mad"? After the explosion, relationships turn sour, and former friends become enemies. The damage is devastating. A rumor runs amuck, an ill-advised leap to a conclusion, a heated overreaction, and boom—an explosion of anger—from the inside.

Anger is a normal human emotion. But *anger* is one letter short of *danger*. The goal is learning to control anger—allowing God to be in control of our emotions—rather than allowing

---

86. Paul Aurandt, *Paul Harvey's The Rest of the Story* (New York: Bantam Books, 1977), 143–145.

anger to control us. Anger also has powerful potential as a force for good—a God-like loving, righteous anger.

In Jonah chapter four, we find a very angry prophet. How could he be fuming with anger after the great awakening in Nineveh? This seems strange, even unthinkable. However, in the sickness of his mind, Jonah claims he had good reason to be angry.

AN EMOTIONAL BREAKDOWN

> It greatly displeased Jonah and he became angry. He prayed to the LORD and said, "Please LORD, was not this what I said while I was still in my own country? Therefore, in order to forestall this, I fled to Tarshish, for I knew that you are a gracious and compassionate God, slow to anger and abundant in loving kindness, and one who relents concerning calamity. "Therefore now, O LORD, please take my life from me, for death is better to me than life." The LORD said, "Do you have good reason to be angry?" … [after the vine withers] Then God said to Jonah, "Do you have good reason to be angry about the plant?" And he said, "I have good reason to be angry, even to death." (Jonah 4:1-4, 9)

Jonah is an emotional mess going through a full-blown meltdown. The two words "greatly displeased" in the first line come from a Hebrew word, *raah*, meaning "to do bad" and "to break down." Jonah is coming unhinged. Deranged. Off his rocker. Nutso. He is burned up about the whole thing. His anger is selfish and sinful.

In addition, four times the word *anger* is used in Jonah 4, a word that means "to burn, to be kindled, to glow, to grow warm. … to become vexed."[87] There is a progression in Jonah's mind

---

87. *Complete Word Study Dictionary* (AMG Publisher, 1994), s.v. "Jonah 4:4, anger."

—first the anger is ignited, and then the more he thinks about it, the hotter he gets until he is in a mad state of mind. His adrenaline is activated so intensely that he crashes into depression and wants to die. A mad person is "mad."

Jonah reminds me of Captain Ahab who lost his leg to the whale Moby Dick in the classic story by the same name. Captain Ahab resolves to do everything in his power to avenge himself on the whale. He is so enraged that he gets crazier and crazier—finally blaming everything that has gone bad since the beginning of time on the whale Moby Dick. I think Jonah has become insanely angry with Ninevites and obsessed with seeing them destroyed.

FUEL FOR ANGER

A variety of circumstances and conditions may cause anger, and understanding the cause is important to managing anger. What was driving Jonah's anger and what triggers the anger we experience?

1. Bitterness and resentment. What was the source of Jonah's deep resentment for the people of Nineveh? Had Jonah been personally wounded by them? Had one of them murdered a member of his family? Of course, we don't know, but there was something very deep-seated in his hatred for Ninevites?

2. An unforgiving spirit. Jonah wanted the city and the people annihilated. The fact that God was willing to forgive them left Jonah burning inside. Of course, Jonah refused to forgive them even though God forgave him for his runaway stint. Sometimes a hurt in the distant past still haunts us and continues to make us angry. We may get upset when others show love and kindness to those who hurt us. We want payback ... not love.

3. Disappointment. The outcome Jonah wanted is not what occurred. In Jonah's twisted mind, God messed things up by forgiving the people in the city of Nineveh. He was disappointed that what he proclaimed didn't happen. Disappointment may leave us vulnerable to anger. We work hard at something, but then things don't turn out the way we wanted. Our disappointment displays itself as anger. We may be disappointed with our self or others who have not measured up. Organizations don't always measure up to our expectations—the company you work for, the church you attend, the grocery store, a website retailer, your bank, or the government.

4. Frustration. Life is exasperating. We don't live in a perfect world. Lines are a reality of life. Traffic isn't going to go away. Getting stuck in a phone tree is maddening. If you're waiting in line and getting frustrated, ask yourself, *Will getting angry change the situation? Is it worth getting upset about?*

5. Conflict. When relating to others, there is potential for friction. A difference of opinion may arise, a disagreement with how money should be spent, conflicting political views, etc. If you are accosted by an angry person who catches you off guard, you may quickly become angry. Sometimes just being around an angry person—even if they don't attack you—will raise your level of anger. Friction may also include an unresolved issue. When someone explodes over a small issue, there is likely an unresolved issue underneath. An irritated comment about "meatloaf again" for dinner may be more about a frustrating day and a run-in with someone at the office than meatloaf.

This is called displacement—an emotion that is repressed when first experienced and then expresses itself later in something unrelated.

6. Fatigue. When you're tired, short on sleep, or physically not feeling well, you are much more likely to get angry. What time of day are you most vulnerable to being irritated, short-tempered? Is your blood sugar low? Eat at regular intervals and get adequate sleep—these are absolutes in managing anger.

7. Fear. When someone feels threatened or worried, anger will surface. If you drive like a maniac or ignore the gas gauge, don't be surprised by the angry response from someone in the car with you. If you're at a party and act foolishly and embarrass the person with you, expect them to react with anger. On the other hand, if you are the one feeling fear or worry, let the person know how their action is affecting you rather than exploding with anger.

8. Hurt feelings. If you hit your thumb with a hammer, you probably say something like, "I perceive that my thumb is quite uncomfortable." Right? No, instead you may be tempted to throw something or say something that will make people wonder if you're a Christian. As physical pain triggers anger, emotional pain causes similar reactions. If we feel rejected, criticized, or misunderstood, agitated feelings will rise, anger will simmer.

9. Faulty perception. Angry emotions have a way of clouding clear thinking. Perception is blurred. Because of anger, we may make distorted assumptions regarding the actions or motives of someone. Prevent false assumptions by asking questions,

152

collecting facts, and withholding a conclusion. Guard against reacting based on faulty information.

10. A wedge to get your own way. A child who wants ice cream in the grocery store may kick and scream to get their own way. When the parent, embarrassed by the child's behavior, gives in and buys them ice cream, the child has learned a technique to get what they want. As this is repeated, the learned behavior becomes more entrenched. Unfortunately, as they get older, they keep using the same methodology. Until someone confronts the angry person who is throwing a fit and refuses to yield, they will continue their childish behavior.

GROWING UP ANGRY

I grew up in a home with angry outbursts and arguments. Dad usually started the day being upset about something: "Where are my socks?" "Who drank all the milk?" "Where are my car keys?" He would stomp around the house letting everyone know how unhappy he was. This affected everyone and set the tone for the day. Finally, with anger adrenaline surging, he would slam the door on the way out. I learned this behavior and assumed the way to get a day's work done was to get angry.

Dad and I would argue about the most senseless issues. I learned early on that I could never win an argument with him. He was a driven workaholic and demanded the same level of performance from me. To try to gain his approval, I became a driven overachiever and perfectionist. Sometimes without warning, my dad's wrath would flare, and he'd whip out his belt and start swinging it every which way. If I could escape, I ran and didn't come home until the early hours of the morning. If I couldn't get away, I hunkered down in a corner trying to protect myself. Since I was often mouthy and stubborn, I honestly felt I deserved what I got.

My brothers would ask in jest, "Are you going to Sunday night at the fights this week?" On Sundays, we were required to go to church in the morning and evening. Afterward, the frustrations from the week hit the fan, and everyone came unglued. Tempers flared, anger spewed, arguments turned into shouting matches, doors were slammed.

When I married, I was determined my home would be different. Reacting to the dysfunction in my family of origin, I became skilled at suppressing my anger. As a pastor, I remember the staff saying they thought I never got angry. I thought this was a compliment. Now I realize how unhealthy this was. There are two dysfunctional ways of dealing with anger: exploding with anger or suppressing it, and I was skilled at both. Now I understand anger from a different perspective. God's Word says, "When you are angry, do not sin, and be sure to stop being angry before the end of the day. Do not give the devil a way to defeat you" (Eph. 4:26-27 NCV). The *New American Standard Bible* translates it this way, "Be angry, and *yet* do not sin; do not let the sun go down on your anger, and do not give the devil an opportunity" (Eph. 4:26-27). Three facts stand out in these verses:

1. Everyone experiences anger ("When you are angry" not "for those who happen to get angry").
2. Anger itself is not sin ("Be angry, and *yet* do not sin").
3. Anger must be dealt with daily, or the devil sets up camp in our life ("do not let the sun go down … do not give the devil an opportunity").

HOW IS ANGER RELATED TO BURNOUT?

> "Therefore now, O LORD, please take my life from me, for death is better to me than life." The LORD said, "Do you have good reason to be angry?"
>
> Then Jonah went out from the city and sat east of it. There he made a shelter for himself and sat under it in the shade until he could see what would happen in the city. So the LORD God appointed a plant and it grew up over Jonah to be a shade over his head to deliver him from his discomfort. And Jonah was extremely happy about the plant. But God appointed a worm when dawn came the next day and it attacked the plant and it withered. When the sun came up God appointed a scorching east wind, and the sun beat down on Jonah's head so that he became faint and begged with all his soul to die, saying, "Death is better to me than life."
>
> Then God said to Jonah, "Do you have good reason to be angry about the plant?" And he said, "I have good reason to be angry, even to death." (Jonah 4:3-9)

Three times Jonah expresses his desire to die. He is as low emotionally as he was in the belly of the fish. His burning anger was accompanied by extreme depression. It is not uncommon for bouts of anger to be followed by feelings of depression. The greater the level of anger, the deeper the depression as in this case of Jonah. However, not all depression is caused by anger.

Burnout and depression are not uncommon in the ministry. More than one-third of pastors are currently at high or medium risk of burnout,[88] and 71 percent report experiencing burnout at some point in their ministry.[89] In addition, almost half of pastors have faced depression at some time during their ministry,[90] and

---

88. David Kinnaman, *The State of Pastors: Barna Report* (Barna Group, 2017), 11, 20–21.

89. "The Results of Our 2016 Pastor Survey," *ExPastors*, Mar. 31, 2019, www.expastors.com/2016-expastors-pastor-survey/.

90. *The State of Pastors: Barna Report*, 2017, 11.

35 percent of pastors are battling depression or fear of inadequacy regularly.[91] Burnout is more often caused by getting "burned up" about something than by long hours and hard work though these take their toll.

The burned-out prophet plants himself on the hillside to see what will happen. He made a shelter, and God graciously provided a vine to provide shade for the stubborn, defiant prophet. The plant is likely the castor oil plant, commonly called "palm-christ" (*palma-christi*). It grows from eight to ten feet high. Only one leaf grows on a branch, but that leaf is often more than twelve inches across. The collective leaves on the various branches provide good shelter from the heat. The plant grows rapidly and fades quickly when injured.[92]

Jonah is very happy about this vine until a small worm comes and destroys the plant. Following this, a scorching east wind comes. This is likely a *sirocco* that comes off the Arabian desert with high velocity and scorching temperatures.

Twice God confronts Jonah: "The LORD said, 'Do you have good reason to be angry?'" (v. 4) and "'Do you have good reason to be angry about the plant?'" (v. 9). The implied answer is no. But is there a time to be angry? Yes. To understand when anger is right and wrong, it will be helpful to understand the different types of anger.

---

91. *Statistics on Pastors: 2016 Update* (Francis A. Schaeffer Institute of Church Leadership Development, 2016), 15, accessed Mar. 31, 2019, https://files.stablerack.com/webfiles/71795/pastorsstatWP2016.pdf.

92. Jamieson, Fausset, & Brown, s.v. "Jonah 4:6."

WHAT ARE THE FOUR TYPES OF ANGER?

In the Bible, there are four different types of anger. Of the four types, one is externally driven, the second is internally driven, the third is concealed, and the fourth is God-driven.

TYPE ONE: IRRITATED ANGER
"I *react* with anger when you …"

If you grew up with siblings, you likely heard the phrase, "You make me so mad!" Early on, we learn to blame others, but in truth, we choose to get angry—and we can choose to ignore it. Anger is our responsibility.

This type of anger usually begins with minor irritations—a put-down, a disagreement, a thoughtless deed—but, such anger can quickly escalate out of control. When we become angry, our body is affected in a variety of ways. For this reason, body language is used to describe the various types of anger. There is a unique word picture and a play on words to describe this first type of anger. This Hebrew word for anger, *aph,* meaning "nose or nostril," is also a word for anger. Notice this play on words: "For the churning of milk produces butter, and pressing the nose (Heb. *aph*) brings forth blood; so the churning of anger (Heb. *aph*) produces strife" (Prov. 30:33, Heb. word supplied).

If someone pops you in the nose, you may get a nose bleed; if someone pops you in your ego, you may get an anger bleed. Type One: Irritated Anger is getting punched-in-the-nose-anger.

Have you ever studied a person's nose when they get fuming mad? Typically, the nose becomes red, and the nostrils flare. You may hear a snort, a sound caused by the force of the breath through the nose that makes a loud, harsh sound. The word *snort,* among its various definitions, also means "to show contempt, defiance, or anger." My uncle's childhood nickname was Snort.

This was long before the days of snorting drugs, and he picked up the tag from his response when angry. His nostrils would flair followed by a harsh, loud, defiant sound of contempt.

In another word picture, Type One: Irritated Anger is described as an "overwhelming flood" (Prov. 27:4 AMP). Anger may begin with a trickle—a minor irritation, a rude comment, a petty disagreement—but then it quickly escalates into a flood. Some event triggers the mind and body to react. There is a flushing of the skin, the muscles become rigid, the jaw tightens, the stomach, shoulders, and hands tighten. There is an adrenaline surge that affects the nervous and muscular systems. Breathing becomes short and rapid.

Out-of-control anger, like mercury in a thermometer, progresses up an emotional escalator.

THE ANGER ESCALATOR

1. Anger begins as a mild annoyance. A feeling of displeasure or uneasiness stirs inside. Here is an opportunity to stop the emotion.

2. Anger moves from annoyance to irritability. The feeling now begins to express itself in touchiness or grumpiness.

3. Anger grows from irritability to seething. Now there is a need to answer back, to avenge, or to hurt in some subtle way.

4. Anger changes from seething to wrath. The feelings now vent themselves. This is the level where you "take the gloves off" so to speak, and the anger spills out.

5. Wrath becomes fury and rage. When you're mad, you're "mad." Getting mad is a form of madness. Rational thinking is blurred, emotions take over, negativity rises, and you will say and do stupid things.

6. Wrath and anger turn to depression. This is the after effect of anger. "We never get angry just once. It's always twice— once at the other person, and later, as we come to our senses, at ourselves."[93]

7. Anger and wrath become a habitual pattern of response. Like the mercury in a thermometer, anger rises and falls, but with each escalation of anger, a pattern is developed that eventually becomes uncontrollable.[94]

Anger may do great damage. Steve Tran of Westminster, California had a cockroach problem in his apartment. He decided to go after them in a "big way" so he set off twenty-five activated bug bombs. According to the *Arizona Republic* (April 25, 1995), when the spray reached the pilot light of the stove, it ignited, setting his furniture on fire, breaking all his windows, and blasting his screen door across the street.

"I really wanted to kill all of them," he said. "I thought if I used a lot more, it would last longer." Two canisters of the fumigant would have been enough for the cockroach problem in Tran's apartment. The blast caused over $10,000 damage to the apartment building.

---

93. David W. Augsburger, *Seventy Times Seven: The Freedom of Forgiveness* (Chicago: Moody Press, 1970), 56.
94. Adapted from an unknown source.

The reporter asked, "What about the cockroaches? Did you get rid of them?" Tran reported, "By Sunday, I saw them walking around."[95]

Conclusion: don't blow your screen door off trying to deal with a cockroach-sized irritation.

TYPE TWO: HABITUAL ANGER
"I *am* angry, and my hot temper may explode …"

In contrast to the first type of anger, "I *react* with anger," this is "I *am* angry." This is an internal explosion. The smallest thing or nothing at all may set it off. In Proverbs 27:3–4, the Type One: Irritated Anger develops like a flood, gathering force and momentum; Type Two: Habitual Anger is fierce, brutal, violent, hot-tempered (Prov. 27:4). Don't get in the way of wrath. You'll pay the price.

As with Type One: Irritated Anger, there is a word picture and a play on words. Type Two: Habitual Anger is the Hebrew word *chemah* meaning "venom or poison," and this is the word used for "hot-tempered wrath." Notice the play on words in these two passages. "The wicked are estranged from the womb; these who speak lies go astray from birth. They have venom (Heb. *chemah*) like the venom (Heb. *chemah*) of a serpent; Like a deaf cobra that stops up its ear, … They sharpen their tongues like a serpent; the poison of a viper (Heb. *chemah*) is under their lips. Selah (Ps. 58:3–4; 140:3, Heb. word supplied).

Here are two observations from this vivid comparative.

---

95. "To Illustrate," *Christianity Today, Leadership Journal: Recommitment & Growth,* Spring 1996, posted April 1, 1996, accessed on Mar. 31, 2019, https://www.christianitytoday.com.

First, habitual anger is developed early, *even* in the womb.

This is part of the sin bent we're born with. Each person has a unique vulnerability, an area where they are most susceptible. Some are wired with a hot temper and easily explode while others are so laid back, they rarely blow off steam.

Second, they speak lies with tongues that are sharpened to poison others.

If not corrected early, this explosive anger becomes habitual, literally capable of ruining careers and destroying lives. Like the cobra that has stopped its ears and will not obey a snake charmer, they are deaf to all appeals and correction. The snake being discussed is believed to be the very poisonous Egyptian cobra.

Hot-tempered people become addicted to blowing their fuse, and those who hang out with them are in danger of becoming addicted as well. Sometimes you don't have a choice, but Scripture counsels, "Don't hang out with angry people; don't keep company with hotheads. Bad temper is contagious—don't get infected" (Prov. 22:24–25 MSG).

One of the most dangerous places today is the home. Domestic violence is one of the most consistently underreported statistics, and yet an estimated 1.3 million women and 835,000 men are physically assaulted by an intimate partner annually in the United States. Witnessing violence between one's parents or caretakers is the strongest risk factor of transmitting violent behavior from one generation to the next, and boys who witness domestic violence are *twice as likely* to abuse their wives and children when they become adults.[96]

---

96. Patricia Tjaden & Nancy Thoennes, U.S. Dep't of Just., NCJ 183781, *Full Report of the Prevalence, Incidence, and Consequences of Intimate Partner Violence Against Women: Findings from the National Violence Against Women Survey, at iv* (2000), accessed Mar. 31, 2019,

Most cases of spousal and child abuse, whether verbal or physical, are Type Two: Habitual Anger that is out of control. When spousal abuse is taking place, the victim often assumes it is Type One: Irritated Anger. For example, if the husband goes into a violent rage, the wife often thinks, *Don't get him upset. Make sure the house is clean, and the kids don't get in the way. Cook a good meal and everything will be ok.* She looks nice and does everything imaginable to please, and when he goes into a rage, she is mystified, hurt, and confused. The pattern is repeated over and over, and she keeps hoping and praying that if she removes the things that set him off, he will be okay. Why doesn't this work? His rage is Type Two: Habitual Anger or hot-tempered wrath—not Type One: Irritated Anger. He could be on a paradise island with absolutely nothing to get upset about and still explode. Why? This wrath is an internal issue, a volcanic-like eruption.

Volcanic eruptions result from magma (molten rock below the ground) usually 30 to 120 miles beneath the surface.

The magma collects in a magma chamber, as the magma accumulates, the pressure inside the chamber increases. When someone has an angry explosion, we say "he blew his top." The hot-tempered person may treat others with a cold contempt—quiet, withdrawn, indifferent one minute and then fuming with rage the next.

Mt. Erebus and its neighbor volcano Mt. Terror are in Antarctica—unlikely places for volcanoes. The freezing cold exterior of Mt. Erebus—it may be minus 40 degrees F with howling winds—belies the presence of the permanent lava lake inside with temperatures between 1,292 and 2,192°F. The mountain may be quiet with only a cloud of steam swirling out of the crater with a strong stench of sulfur, but without warning, the mountain erupts, blasting lava bombs high in the air.

---

http://www.ojp.usdoj.gov/nij/pubs-sum/183781.htm.

How do you help a hot-tempered person?

First, you cannot rescue them.
"Hot-tempered (Heb. *chemah*) people must pay the penalty. If you rescue them once, you will have to do it again" (Prov. 19:19 NLT, Heb. word supplied). Underline these crucial words. Don't make excuses for them, don't rescue them, don't tell the police it was no big thing, don't refuse to press charges when they have gone on a rampage of violence. They *must* pay the penalty.

Second, the volcanic-like magma chamber must be drained.
Ecclesiastes 7:9 says, "Anger resides in the bosom of fools." Notice the anger is welled up inside them. They live angry. They need a skilled pastor or therapist who can help them deal with the cause of their anger.

TYPE THREE: PASSIVE-AGGRESSIVE ANGER
"I *act* angry though I'd never say so."

This type of anger is subtle and powerful. Some have used passive-aggressive behavior so long as a wedge to get their own way, they aren't even aware of it. Skilled and clever, they can usually get their own way—and if they don't, they can make you feel guilty—and if that doesn't work, they store it away as blame-casting ammunition. This passive-aggressive person may be very charming and pleasant until something doesn't go their way, and then they open their trusty toolbox and get out their sharpened "PA Tool." They are skilled at silent seething, displaying a "poor-me-how-could-you-do-this-to-me-you-terri-ble-awful-person" attitude.

How does passive-aggressive behavior develop? Clever and veiled, it begins with an inability or reluctance to express anger acceptably. They may have been brought up in a home where it was wrong to be angry, so they learned to use actions to speak louder than words—learning to sulk or pout. Rather than putting up a fuss if they didn't want to do something, they would procrastinate and drag their feet for as long as possible. When frustrated, they would become sullen and silent. Punishing others with the silent treatment was a way of getting to other people without saying a word. Bottom line: passive-aggressive behavior says, "Don't cross me, or you will pay."

Irritated that his wife told him the kitchen sink needed repair just as he was leaving to play golf with the guys on Saturday morning, he thinks, *How dare she lay a guilt trip on me just as I was going to play golf.* To get back at her, he is cold and distant when he gets home. And he procrastinates on fixing the leaky sink. Drip, drip, drip. She is angry that the leak hasn't been repaired, so she serves meals a half hour to forty-five minutes late as she thinks to herself, *I'll show him.* They are both practicing "mutism"—punishing with an absence of words. Those who engage in passive-aggressive behavior justify it by casting blame rather than owning up to their responsibility. Many of us employ some shade of it—often quite unaware we're doing it. This is a good time to identify and correct it.

Sounding like an oxymoron or a contradiction, passive-aggressive is a current term for behavior that has been practiced for centuries. The biblical word that most closely correlates is "provocation" (Heb. word *kaas*) which means "to be angry, to be gloomy, heavily weighted, depressed, sullen, and to provoke others to anger." Inside, the passive-aggressive person is stewing, and they use their sullen behavior to provoke anger or lay a heavy trip on others.

Solomon, whose many wives and mistresses turned his heart away from God, may have been thinking of one of his passive-aggressive wives when he said, "It is better to live in a desert land than with a contentious and vexing woman" (Prov. 21:19). The word "vexing" is this word provocation or anger—a gloomy, depressed passive-aggressive person who makes others feel guilty with their anger. *The Message Bible* describes her as "a cross and petulant spouse"—meaning irritable over trifles, cranky, crabby, peevish, grumpy. I say, "Serves the guy right for having all those wives and mistresses." Amen, anyone? Let's be fair, I think it is better to live in a swamp than with a quarrelsome, grumpy, and cranky husband.

This word for passive-aggressive anger is the word *annoyance* in this passage, "A fool shows his annoyance at once, but a prudent man overlooks an insult" (Prov. 12:16). The foolish person acts out—displaying passive-aggressive behavior, so everyone knows they are annoyed. The wise person overlooks an insult.

This third type of anger also has a word picture. While in grade school, my brothers, and I went rock hunting with my dad in the rugged country below Yellowstone and east of the Grand Tetons in Wyoming. Hiking back into the little-explored territory, we were excited with each piece of petrified wood or stalactite we found. Our eyes were bigger than our backs. By late afternoon, we had amassed a large collection, and we had to trek back to camp. We were exhausted, and those rocks weren't nearly so exciting now that we had to carry them. We groaned and moaned, and then tried to load them in my dad's backpack. He would quickly say, "If you want it, you carry it."

Passive-aggressive anger is described as "heavy"—as a backpack of heavy rocks. Those using it lay a "heavy" on others—a backpack of guilt like a backpack full of rocks. To stop their subtle scheming, expose what they are doing. Cut them off at the pass. Tell the person trying to use passive-aggressive on you, "Don't try to lay a heavy on me. You can try to make me feel guilty, but I'm not going to accept that."

All three types of anger are in this passage—each with a comparative to help understand it. "A stone is heavy and the sand weighty, but the *provocation* (type three: passive-aggressive anger) of a fool is heavier than both of them. *Wrath* (type two: habitual anger) is fierce and *anger* (type one: irritated anger) is a flood," (Prov. 27:3–4, explanation and emphasis supplied).

If you want to explore this further in the New Testament, there are three Greek words used for anger that are closely equivalent: (1) type one anger (*orge),* to make angry, to have an orgy; (2) type two rage (*thumos),* hot wrath, rage, a violent wind or passion; and (3) type three bitterness, (*pikria),* to be bitter, to cut, to act out. For example, Ephesians 4:31 uses these three words for anger: "Let all bitterness (type three, *pikria*) and wrath (type two, *thumos*) and anger (type one, *orge*), … be put away from you" (Eph. 4:31, emphasis and explanation supplied).

Instead of being angry, "Be kind to one another, tender-hearted, forgiving each other, just as God in Christ also has forgiven you" (Eph. 4:32).

If you stuff your anger and hold it inside, never speaking up, it's likely to leak out in other ways. Your health will be affected—headaches, body aches and pains, digestive issues, and decreased immunity to sickness—to name a few.

TYPE FOUR: RIGHTEOUS ANGER
"I *grieve* over the things that grieve the heart of God."

Anger is God-given emotional energy, and God doesn't forbid it. Most of us associate anger with inappropriate behavior, and as a result, we fail to identify the tremendous power and potential for good in Type Four: Righteous Anger. Psalm 4:4 says, "Tremble (or be angry), and do not sin; Meditate in your heart upon your bed and be still. Selah." This word for anger (Heb. *rāgaz*) means "to shake or to tremble." Have you ever experienced anger that caused you to tremble or shake? This word for anger occurs forty-one times in the Old Testament and frequently expresses the idea of the physical moving or shaking of someone or something. Lands (1 Sam. 14:15; Amos 8:8), mountains (Ps. 18:7; Isa. 5:25), the heavens (2 Sam. 22:8), kingdoms (Isa. 23:11), and even the whole earth (Joel 2:10) are described as being shaken in this way, with the Lord's anger often given as the basis for the quaking. On a human level, people, whether groups or individuals, would shake, i.e., were moved or stirred by deep emotions in response to specific circumstances.[97]

Each of the four types of anger contains a word picture. **Type One: Irritated Anger** is getting punched-in-the-nose anger; **Type Two: Habitual Anger** is like the venom of a snake, **Type Three: Passive-aggressive Anger** is laying a heavy on someone like a load of heavy rocks; and **Type Four: Righteous Anger** is picture of shaking and trembling. Imagine God-empowered shaking—a moving of lands, kingdoms, mountains, the heavens, and the whole earth. **Righteous anger bears little resemblance to our self-centered skirmishes, turf wars, and fits of anger.**

Jesus was angry—displaying powerful, righteous indignation for the temple money changers who were like the Jerusalem Mafia. This occurred twice: once at the beginning of his ministry (John 2:13–16) and again on Monday of the week of his crucifixion. "Jesus entered the temple and drove out all those who were buying and selling in the temple and overturned the tables of the money changers and the seats of those who were

---

97. *Complete Word Study Dictionary* (AMG Publisher, 1994), s.v. "Joel 2:10, quake: *ragaz*."

selling doves. And He said to them, 'It is written, MY HOUSE SHALL BE CALLED A HOUSE OF PRAYER; but you are making it a ROBBERS' DEN'" (Matt. 21:12–13).

Before identifying why Jesus turned tables over in anger, we should understand what was going on that was *right*. The collecting of the temple tax of a half shekel was called for in Exodus 30:13. The changing of money from one currency to another was allowed according to the Talmud (63 books interpreting the Old Testament), and the offering of animal sacrifices was prescribed in Numbers 28:16–25. The exchanging of money or selling of doves were not wrong.

What was *wrong*? With the noise of oxen, sheep, doves and the shouts of hucksters, the rattle of coins, and voices raised in bargaining disputes, no one could worship in the Court of the Gentiles. It must have resembled a stockyard with the stench, filth, bleating, and lowing of animals. The money changers, sitting cross-legged behind their little coin-covered tables, were ripping the people off. Only Jewish coins were allowed in the temple, and the money changers would charge as much as a day's wages for currency exchange. Also, the temple merchants charged about one-fourth of a day's wages to inspect animals, and the worshipper was usually told his animal was unacceptable. Then they had to buy an "acceptable animal" at rip-off prices. The dove was one of the acceptable offerings usually selected by the poor. They had to pay up to twenty times the normal price for a dove. They were as corrupt as the Roman tax gatherers. This was the Jerusalem Mafia ripping the people off.[98]

***

98. William Barclay, *The Daily Study Bible: The Gospel of John,* Vol. 1 (Philadelphia: Westminster Press, 1955), 95–98.

No wonder Jesus hit this place and hit it hard. With whips, he turned tables over and took on the corruption in the house of God. I become angry reading about it.

Righteous anger fueled Martin Luther at the selling of indulgences—a full or partial remission of temporal punishment due for sins which have already been forgiven. In 1831, Abraham Lincoln visited New Orleans. This was his first time seeing the horrors of slavery up close. His soul was moved with righteous anger when he saw slaves chained, whipped, and auctioned. To those with him, he exclaimed, "By God, boys, let's get away from this. If ever I get a chance to hit that thing [meaning slavery], I'll hit it hard."[99] Thirty-two years later, during the Civil War, he issued the Emancipation Proclamation freeing all the slaves.

The Bible says, "BE ANGRY, AND YET DO NOT SIN; do not let the sun go down on your anger, and do not give the devil an opportunity" (Eph. 4:26–27). This is a "permissive imperative" according to A. T. Robertson, one of the finest Greek scholars of the twentieth century.[100] In other words, don't go around looking for things to get angry about, but instead, if you do see injustice and wrong, it is permissible and imperative to "be angry, but do not sin." Philosopher Aristotle (384–322 BC) said it this way, "Anybody can become angry—that is easy, but to be angry with the right person and to the right degree and at the right time and for the right purpose, and in the right way—that is not within everybody's power and is not easy."[101]

---

99. William H. Herndon and Jesse W. Weik, *Herndon's Life of Abraham Lincoln* (Cleveland: World Publishing Co., 1943), 63–64.

100. A. T. Robertson, *Word Pictures in the New Testament* (Nashville: Broadman Press, 1932, database *WordSearch*: 2012), s.v. "Eph. 4:26."

101. Aristotle, *Nicomachean Ethics*, 1109a25.

HOW CAN A LOVING GOD BE ANGRY?

Our thoughts of anger are so tainted with sin, we have difficulty reconciling the two. The Bible says, "The LORD is compassionate and gracious, Slow to anger and abounding in lovingkindness" (Ps. 103:8). Numerous times, the Bible says God is "slow to anger," and we are told to be God-like by being "slow to anger." I admit God is much slower to anger than I am.

It was about 10:30 p.m. when I heard a knock on the door. I answered to see one of my best friends. He said, "Could we talk?" I said, "Certainly, come on in."

He proceeded to say, "I am angry, deeply grieving." He was not being attacked, he was not ticked off, he was not fuming. He was grieved and angry about the promiscuous lifestyle of a dad who was ruining his children. Both children were deeply scarred. The situation was a horrible mess. He explained, "I love this dad and his children deeply. It grieves me and makes me angry to see all the hurt and pain." After he left, I thought to myself, *I understand a little better now how a holy God can be angry and totally loving at the same time.*

If you have not received Christ as your Lord and Savior, the wrath of God abides on you, and he loves you deeply—both at the same time. Thankfully, he is slow to anger. Once you place your faith in Christ and receive his forgiveness, the wrath of God for your sins is removed.

As we deal with our dilemma of "I Love the World—It's People I Can't Stand," we may find the behavior of some people so despicable we boil with righteous anger. The rapist, the terrorist, the pimp, and the neo-Nazi do things that are beyond horrible. Righteous anger at their horrible behavior is both fitting and required. But at this point, with our anger rising, we allow the love of God to see beyond their deeds to their desperate condition and lostness. This is "loving the world *and* the people we can't stand." "For God presented Jesus as the sacrifice for sin. People are made right with God when they believe that Jesus sacrificed his life, shedding his blood. This sacrifice shows that God was being fair when he held back and did not punish those who sinned in times past" (Rom. 3:25 NLT).

Think back to your last experience of anger. What kind was it? Irritated anger, habitual anger, passive-aggressive anger, or righteous anger? How did you express it? Or did you repress it? How did you feel two days later? This next section connects the how-to for controlling and properly releasing anger.

HOW TO DO A "CONTROLLED RELEASE" OF ANGER

Anger is powerful stuff and toxic to the human system. Like a buildup in a pressure cooker on the kitchen stove, anger requires a release. I have often thought controlling anger was the most important thing. I still think control is crucial, but now I think of it more like a controlled release. If you constantly tell yourself, *Don't be angry, keep it under control,* pressure builds up inside. This accumulation of high-powered "anger energy" will either fester inside, leak out in insidious ways, or explode like a volcano. Too many are attempting to control anger but becoming highly frustrated. *The controlled release of anger is the key to effective anger management.*

The controlled release involves two different scenarios. The first is what I call the "angry mindset" versus the "angry moment." When I am upset about something (an "angry mindset"), I have time to slow it down, think it through logically, pray, and choose what steps to take.

Anger also has problem-solving potential. As we learn a controlled release of anger, we learn to be assertive. Properly utilized, assertiveness can be logical, compassionate, and creative—not emotionally driven. Calmly, without venom or hostility, the wife can say, "I'm disappointed the leaky sink is not getting repaired. Can you give me a realistic timeline, or would you rather I call a plumber?" He can clarify his feelings by saying, "I was put off when you brought this up as I was leaving to play golf with the guys. It would help me if you jot a note about it, and I'll get to it after my round of golf."

The "angry moment" is when we're caught in the crossfire … sometimes quite unexpectedly. You're having a nice conversation and suddenly hit a topic that stirs strong disagreement. Or you're at a family gathering, and one of your relatives takes a potshot at you. You're blindsided by it, and anger begins escalating. In the "angry moment," you don't have time to analyze the situation or look up scriptures to guide your response. The dark storm clouds have moved in, the wind has picked up, the lightning is flashing from the clouds. Now, what do you do? Here is how to practice a controlled release of anger.

1. Ask God to take control before anger takes control.

Anger marches into your mind demanding control. Respond with an immediate emergency prayer, *Lord, anger is stirring in me. I ask you to control me and my response in this situation.*

2. Take responsibility for your anger.

Fools give full vent to their anger. As Proverbs 29:11 says, "A fool always loses his temper, but a wise man holds it back." Don't blame someone else for making you angry. No one can make you angry unless you allow it. Be a wise person and take control of your anger.

3. Learn to ignore petty disagreements.

"Keeping away from strife is an honor for a man, but any fool will quarrel" (Prov. 20:3). What issues are worth going to the wall for? And what issues are not worth fighting for? If you expend all your energy fighting petty issues, you won't have the energy to fight the big causes. In the church, there are issues that I will fight for—the virgin birth of Jesus Christ, the inspiration of scripture, the deity of Jesus Christ, the Trinity, salvation by faith alone, and similar issues. There are hundreds of issues I won't go to the wall for—like the color of the carpet, styles of music, the frequency of washing the windows, dress or attire in church, etc.

4. Listen.

"Fools think their own way is right, but the wise listen to others" (Prov. 12:15 NLT). You can help take control of a situation with a clarifying question. "If I understand correctly, you are upset because …" or "Can you help me understand your concern a little better?"

5. Slow your anger down by relaxing the attitude and body.

"A wise man controls his temper. He knows that anger causes mistakes. A relaxed attitude lengthens a man's life; …" (Prov. 14:29–30 TLB). If you sit down and relax your body as much as possible, you will find it will help control your emotions. Unfold your arms and open your stance. Take a long, slow breath to slow your pulse. Count to 100.

6. Speak softly.

If they demand a response, speak softly and sincerely. Don't use sarcasm. "A gentle answer turns away wrath, but a harsh word stirs up anger" (Prov. 15:1). Never underestimate the power of the soft-spoken word. "Soft speech breaks down the most bonelike resistance" (Prov. 25:15 AMP). Be honest but loving. "Speak the truth in love" (Eph. 4:15 NLT).

7. Simmer down before the sun goes down.

Having someone unload anger on you, inevitably stirs feelings. Going to bed with anger stewing inside is a guarantee for a horrible night of sleep. If possible, talk your feelings through with someone before bedtime. If you've had an argument, go the person and make things right. "I'm sorry about the things I said. Please forgive me." "Don't stay angry. Don't go to bed angry" (Eph. 4:26 MSG).

When someone gets your ire up, and you're thinking, *You make me so mad,* stop long enough to Remember the *Maine.* Don't have an internal explosion. Don't fight a needless war. Take a deep breath and choose not to ride the anger escalator. Relax. A long walk is a great way to calm a short temper.

The more anger towards the past you carry in your heart, the less capable you are of loving in the present.
—Barbara De Angelis[102]

102. De Angelis, *Brainy Quotes,* accessed Mar. 31, 2019, https://www.brainyquote.com/quotes/barbara_de_angelis_148247.

TIME OUT

CHAPTER SIX

THIS MAKES ME SO MAD

A fool always loses his temper, but a wise man holds it back. (Prov. 29:11)

A gentle answer turns away wrath, but a harsh word stirs up anger. (Prov. 15:1)

GROW AND APPLY

◊ Read Jonah 4:1–4 and Ephesians 4:25–32.

◊ What ticks you off?

_____

_____

_____

_____

_____

_____

◊ When are you most prone to become angry?

_____

_____

_____

_____

_____

_____

◊ Use the worksheet on the following page to process angry feelings and practice a controlled release of anger.

WORKSHEET

Practicing a "Controlled Release" of Anger

(duplicate copies of this worksheet as needed)

1. Identify an area of frustration or anger.

_____

_____

_____

2. What type of anger is it?

_____

- **Type One: Irritated Anger**—"I *react* with anger when …"
- **Type Two: Habitual Anger**—"I *am* angry and fear that I may explode."
- **Type Three: Passive-aggressive Anger**—"I *act* angry though I'd never say so."
- **Type Four: Righteous Anger**—"I *grieve* over the things that grieve the heart of God."

3. Take responsibility for your anger (no one can make you angry—it is a choice to be angry).

4. Journal your thoughts or share with a trusted friend.

I become angry when …

_____

_____

_____

I feel …

_____

_____

_____

_____

_____

I choose to take this action …

_____

_____

_____

_____

_____

_____

Note: if you are experiencing spousal anger to the point of abuse, seek counsel. If you are being physically harmed, leave the home and stay someplace where you are safe.

PRAY

◊ Jesus said, "'You have heard that it was said, 'You shall love your neighbor and hate your enemy.' but I say to you, love your enemies and pray for those who persecute you'" (Matt. 5:43–44).

◊ Pray for anyone who has it in for you or you find difficult to love.

_____

_____

_____

_____

_____

_____

SHARE

Look for opportunities to share your faith. Here are a couple of thought-provoking questions to ask when the time is right.

1. What is frustrating in your life? What ticks you off?
2. What condition in our world grieves you? Does it make you angry?
3. What is the best solution for the ills of our world?

TIME TOGETHER

CHAPTER SIX

THIS MAKES ME SO MAD

If you're leading a small group, teaching a Bible class, or sharing with the family, below are some opening questions. For the content of the lesson, use the Grow and Apply, Prayer, and Share sections with your Time Out.

CONNECT
(choose one or two for discussion)

◊ How did your family of origin handle anger?

_____

_____

_____

_____

◊ How has this affected you today?

_____

_____

_____

_____

_____

_____

CHAPTER SEVEN

WHAT MATTERS MOST

I was leading in the closing prayer on Sunday evening, March 16, 1986. The day had been a long but thrilling. That evening, we had our church vision dinner. We focused on the needs of our community, and everyone felt excited about the new plans for evangelism. My closing prayer began, "Lord, we thank you for all your goodness and the joyous time we have had today …" And as I focused on the lost we hoped to reach, I concluded my prayer: "… and may the saved get lost. Amen." There was a chuckle rippling through the crowd before everyone burst into laughter.

This is where we find Jonah: "… and may the saved get lost!"

Jonah was a great success! Or was he? Jonah scored big in terms of numbers. The entire city of Nineveh—perhaps a million people or more—repented. But in God's evaluation of success, Jonah was a zero—without love for people. Jonah was lacking what matters most. Instead of showing compassion and love for the people of Nineveh, Jonah was feeling sorry for himself.

HOW TO THROW A PITY PARTY ... AND WHAT TO EXPECT

Most of us have thrown a pity party in honor of the big three—me, myself, and I. We are gloomy over something—a loss, a rejection, a lingering bitterness. Follow the pattern of Jonah, and you too can have your own pity party. But be prepared for the consequences. Here's a step-by-step guide to being miserable.

1. Set up your self-centered shelter where you can sulk.

Longing for the destruction of Nineveh, "Jonah went out from the city and sat east of it. There he made a shelter for himself and sat under it in the shade until he could see what would happen in the city" (Jonah 4:5).

Jonah builds a shelter to shield himself from the sun. Nothing wrong with that considering the scorching temperatures in that part of the world. He came into the city from the west and exited to the east side of the city. Archaeologists have discovered a large mound, known as *Kuyunjik*, that rises about ninety feet and overlooks the city—possibly where Jonah set up his shelter. This unhappy camper erects his booth with a city view. He was probably mumbling to himself, *I can't believe God would forgive them. They deserve judgment—not mercy. This is unfair. I want them destroyed.*

Jonah's focus: "It's all about me." In his little shelter, he pouts.

You can set up your own place to sulk—the coffee shop, the bar, a hillside, the back room of your home. It's all about isolation. Sing the blues, mope, feel sorry for yourself, and satiate your senses with what little pleasure you can find.

2. Seek happiness in what is unimportant.

While Jonah is sulking in his shelter, "The Lord God appointed a plant and it grew up over Jonah to be a shade over his head to deliver him from his discomfort. And Jonah was extremely happy about the plant" (Jonah 4:6).

Notice the word "appointed" (v. 6). In the book of Jonah, God appointed the fish (1:17), the vine (4:6), the worm (4:7), and the wind (4:8). Everything God appointed, obeyed—except Jonah. In the entire universe, there are only two rebels: fallen man and fallen angels. Everything else in the created world gives glory to God. God was making divine appointments—just as he appoints people and circumstances in your life to shape and mature you. God was in charge—make no mistake about it.

God graciously provides a vine to shield Jonah from the sun and ease his discomfort. Was it a gourd, or castor bean, or castor oil plant? Traditionally, many thought a gourd fit the description best. When Jerome changed the traditional identification of the plant from the gourd to the castor oil plant, it caused a riot in Carthage.[103] The "gourd crowd" rioted over a gourd? How ridiculous!

After studying the gourd as well as the castor bean plant, I think the latter fits the description best. Castor bean plants grow to over twelve feet in the Middle East. With large shade-giving leaves, they grow quickly, lengthening themselves by as much as twelve to eighteen inches a day. They also wither quickly when attacked at their base by insects like wireworms.[104] There is nothing wrong with Jonah being happy about the shade tree. God provided the vine as a blessing. The sad part is this: *this is*

---

103. Gaebelein, *Expositor's Bible Commentary*, Vol. 7, 387.
104. *Zondervan Pictorial Encyclopedia*, Vol. 2 (Grand Rapids, MI: Zondervan Publishing House, 1976), s.v. "gourd."

the only thing in the book that makes Jonah happy. The evangelist should be doing cartwheels and jumping with the angels over the repentance and great awakening in a city of a million or more.

When we're into our pity party, we major in trivial things—unimportant. We may immerse ourselves in TV, computer games, the internet, or bingeing on food. God has a way of dealing with these issues.

3. Don't be surprised when God shatters your idol.

When something in life becomes more important than God, he may shatter it. If plants become more important than people, will they wither and die? This was the case for Jonah. "God appointed a worm when dawn came the next day and it attacked the plant and it withered" (Jonah 4:7).

"Though not expressly stated, the action Jonah took to 'ease his discomfort' likely occurred in the hot season, when the mean daily maximum temperature in Mesopotamia is about 110 degrees Fahrenheit."[105] Jonah is cooked, calloused, and angry. He has no friends and hates Ninevites. George Addison said, "Three grand essentials to happiness in this life are something to do, something to love, and something to hope for."[106] Jonah has none of these essentials. Jonah is alone and out of fellowship with God. So, he gets attached to a castor bean plant.

We can get attached to some strange and worthless things. In the process of brokenness, God may shatter an idol we've set up—anything that takes precedence over God in our lives.

---

105. Gaebelein, *Expositor's Bible Commentary*, Vol. 7, 387.
106. Joseph Addison, *Brainy Quote*, accessed Mar. 31, 2019, https://www.brainyquote.com/quotes.

4. When you're "burned up" over something, you'll soon be "burned out."

Everything is hot—the sun, the wind, Jonah's head, and his temper. "When the sun came up God appointed a scorching east wind, and the sun beat down on Jonah's head so that he became faint and begged with all his soul to die, saying, 'Death is better to me than life.'" (Jonah 4:8).

As I mentioned earlier, the "scorching east wind" fits the description of the sirocco winds. Dennis Baly comments about the sirocco winds that blow across Iraq from the southeast usually accompanied by a huge wind-driven sand storm. "During the period of the sirocco the temperature rises steeply, sometimes even climbing during the night, and it remains high, about 16–22 degrees F. above the average ... at times every scrap of moisture seems to have been extracted from the air, so that one has the curious feeling that one's skin has been drawn much tighter than usual. Sirocco days are peculiarly trying to the temper and tend to make even the mildest people irritable and fretful and to snap at one another for apparently no reason at all."[107]

If Jonah lost all his hair from the acid in the fish, his bald head must have been like a frying pan. A hothead, hot temper, and the hot winds bring Jonah to a boiling point: "Death is better to me than life" (Jonah 4:8).

What causes burnout? Long hours and hard work may be a factor, but the biggest contributor to burn out is getting burned up about some issue. This fries the emotional circuitry faster than anything I know. Even after the anger subsides, you will feel exhausted, depleted, and unable to carry on. When you blow a

---

107. Dennis Baly, *The Geography of the Bible* (London: Lutterworth, 1957), 67–68.

fuse and explode with anger, you can expect to feel depressed and burned out a short time later.

5. Expect to be miserable.

Confronted in his miserable state, "God said to Jonah, 'Do you have good reason to be angry about the plant?' And he said, 'I have good reason to be angry, even to death.'" (Jonah 4:9). Jonah responds to God's question: "You bet, I've got good reason to be exceedingly angry!" "He responded sharply with what was most likely a Hebrew expletive."[108] His response was something like, "You're damn right. I've got good reason to be angry."

Jonah's soul is like his scorched body—burned out. He expresses his desire to die three times.

> "Therefore now, O Lord, please take my life from me, for death is better to me than life." (v. 3)

> "Death is better to me than life." (v. 8)

> "I have good reason to be angry, even to death." (Jonah 4:9)

Throwing a pity party is a gradual descent into an emotional abyss. But there is hope. The Psalmist David called out to God, "'Rescue me from the swamp, don't let me go under for good, … This whirlpool is sucking me down'" (Ps. 69:14 MSG). God will rescue you from an emotional pit when you call on him.

WHAT REALLY MATTERS?

It doesn't matter how big a house you live in, how nice a car you drive, how many awards and plaques are on your wall, how much applause you receive, how many books you have written,

---

108. John H. Walton, *Bible Study Commentary: Jonah* (Grand Rapids: Zondervan Publishing House, 1982), 60.

how many countries you've traveled to, how many degrees you've earned. *It doesn't matter.*

What matters is love.

If you live a life of loving God and people, you are a success— in God's eyes. When we sort everything out, what else really matters?

How do people describe you? Good speaker, great musician, skilled craftsman, awesome cook, amazing organizer, charming personality, etc. These are heartwarming, feel-good affirmations— nothing wrong with them. But the ultimate compliment is when people say, "He or she is one of the most loving people I have ever met."

While Jonah is wallowing in self-pity, God asks him if he couldn't at least care for the innocent children and the animals in Nineveh. "Then the LORD said, 'You had compassion on the plant for which you did not work and which you did not cause to grow, which came up overnight and perished overnight. Should I not have compassion on Nineveh, the great city in which there are more than 120,000 persons who do not know the difference between their right and left hand, as well as many animals?'" (Jonah 4:10–11).

What is meant by 120,000 who can't tell their right hand from their left? This is not the population of the city. Instead, God is referring to 120,000 innocent children—likely preschool age. Since there are 120,000 preschool-age children, what is the population of the city? In the US 2000 Census, 3.49 percent of the population was between the ages 0–4.[109] If 3.49 percent of Nineveh's population had been children ages 0–4, it would have meant a population of about 3.5 million people which seems

---

109. "United States Age Distribution, 2000," *CensusScope*, accessed Mar. 31, 2019, http://www.censusscope.org/us/chart_age.html.

unlikely. In general, families were larger in those times, and people didn't live as long. To be conservative, if 10 percent of the population of Nineveh were children ages 0–4, the population of the city would be about 1.2 million. Commentators Jamieson, Fausset, and Brown concur: "Jonah (Jonah 4:11) mentions the children as numbering one hundred twenty thousand, which would give about a million to the whole population."[110] This seems to be a reasonable estimate of the population.

Jonah was focused on himself—his love for God and others was a zero. What a difference between Jesus and Jonah. Jonah said, "I am angry enough to die." Jesus said, "I love you so much I am willing to die." His love demonstrated ultimate love. In 1 Corinthians 13, the great love chapter, we discover what is meaningless if not done in love.[111]

WITHOUT LOVE, IT DOESN'T MATTER HOW GREAT A COMMUNICATOR YOU ARE.

> If I could speak in any language in heaven or on earth but didn't love others, I would only be making meaningless noise like a loud gong or a clanging cymbal. (1 Cor. 13:1 NLT)

Paul certainly had in mind the heathen worship that was characterized by the clashing and the clanging of cymbals. Gong, gong, clang, clang … annoying, meaningless. Reminds me of the old "Gong Show" when you were "gonged" if your performance was awful.

We like to hear good speakers—communicators. We applaud eloquence and charisma. Nothing you or I say will matter if we

110. Jamieson, Fausset, and Brown, s.v. "Jonah 3:3."
111. Some of the thoughts in the following section were adapted from Rick Warren, *40 Days of Love: What Matters Most,* Oct. 13, 2001.

don't live a life of love. You may speak five or six languages. You may be an awesome communicator. You may be a great debater. It is all a zero without love.

WITHOUT LOVE, IT DOESN'T MATTER HOW GIFTED YOU ARE OR HOW MUCH YOU KNOW.

> If I had the gift of prophecy, and if I understood all of God's secret plans and possessed all knowledge ... (1 Cor. 13:2 NLT)

People are pursuing advanced degrees at a frenzied pace. Our society worships at the shrine of knowledge. Buckminster Fuller created the "Knowledge Doubling Curve" indicating that in 1900 human knowledge doubled approximately every 100 years. Daniel predicted that in the end times, knowledge and travel would vastly increase (Dan. 12:4). By the end of World War II, knowledge was doubling every twenty-five years. With the explosion of the computer age and the internet "... on average human knowledge is doubling every 13 months."[112] This is astounding, but we still have the same problems of war, crime, terrorism, racism, and hatred.

What is needed most? More knowledge? Paul said, "Knowledge puffs you up with pride, but love builds up" (1 Cor. 8:1 NCV). Love is what the world needs most.

You may be a genius, brilliant, a walking encyclopedia of information, and have awesome insights into spiritual truth, but without love, it amounts to zilch—nothing.

---

112. David Russell Schilling, "Knowledge Doubling Every 12 Months, Soon to be Every 12 Hours," *Industry Tap*, April 19, 2013 accessed Mar. 31, 2019, http://www.industrytap.com/knowledge-doubling-every-12-months-soon-to-be-every-12-hours/3950.

WITHOUT LOVE, IT DOESN'T MATTER HOW BIG YOUR VISION OR GREAT YOUR FAITH.

If I had such faith that I could move mountains, but didn't love others, I would be nothing. (1 Cor. 13:2 NLT)

You may have a great vision for ministry and the ability to believe God for things that others can't. You may have thousands of people following your leadership. Without love, it is a zero.

WITHOUT LOVE, IT DOESN'T MATTER HOW MUCH YOU ACHIEVE OR GIVE.

If I gave everything I have to the poor and even sacrificed my body, I could boast about it; but if I didn't love others, I would have gained nothing. (1 Cor. 13:3 NLT)

You can accomplish great things—build a booming company, make astounding discoveries, be recognized as one of the great achievers in your field, give millions to charitable causes—but it counts for nothing without love. Giving great sums of money or possessions may be done for selfish reasons. Some people give to get something back or because they feel guilty. Others give to control things or to receive recognition. As Amy Carmichael, missionary to India for fifty-five years, said, "You can give without loving, but you cannot love without giving."

You can invest yourself in a great spiritual ministry and see hundreds come to Christ, but if it is not done with love, it counts for nothing.

Evangelist Jack Holcomb tells of the time he was in Denver speaking to overflow crowds. The response was so great that he had to extend the crusade three days. This made him pressed for time to get to his next crusade in southern Colorado. After his last message in Denver, he jumped in his car, exhausted and stressed for time, and headed south.

Just a few miles out of town he saw those telltale flashing red lights in his rearview mirror. He pulled to the side of the road, upset and tired, jumped out of the car, and snapped at the highway patrolman, "Okay, I was speeding, just give me the stupid ticket ... I don't know why cops don't have something better do like catching real criminals instead of harassing motorists ..." As he spoke, he got more and more upset. "Just hurry up and write the dumb ticket!"

The officer, who had been quietly listening, said, "Wait, wait ... you know, I used to be a lot like you are ... angry, snapping at people ... but four days ago I was attending a series of meetings in Denver, and I heard about someone who could change my life, and before we talk about the ticket, let me tell you about someone who can change your life as well ... his name is Jesus Christ."

As you might imagine, Holcomb was looking around for a hole to hide in, but he dared to look the police officer in the eye and say, "I'm the man who told you about Christ, and I'm ashamed."[113] He took his glasses off and wept.

Jonah had just led one of the greatest crusades of all time, and now he is a grumpy, grouchy, angry prophet. Jonah scored big time in terms of numbers, but without love, Jonah was a zero.

WHAT IS LOVE?

Confusion is rampant when it comes to understanding love. Love is a dangerously misused word; we use it for all kinds of

---

113. "Lessons in Thinking—and Feeling—Before Saying Hurtful Things," *Gilroy Dispatch,* accessed Mar. 31, 2019, http://www.gilroy-dispatch.com.

things. We love ice cream, we love our dog or cat, we love a singer we've never met, we love our car or stereo system, and we use the same word to express the lifetime commitment to the one we care about more than anyone else in the world. If you look up love in the twenty-two-volume print edition of *World Book Encyclopedia*, you won't find a single article. It simply says, "See sex, emotions." The Greeks wisely distinguished different types of love by using four different words.[114]

Biological love

The Greeks used the word *storgē* or *stergein* from which we get the word "stork." This is family love, the natural love of parents for their children, children for their parents, grandparents for their grandchildren, love of a husband and wife since they are one flesh, and a healthy and appropriate love between brothers and sisters. This is a love that's based in one's own nature, biologically rooted from shared genetics. It's non-sexual.

Friendship love

The Greeks used the word *phileō* (from which we get the name Philadelphia, the city of brotherly love) to describe the shared friendship between two people. Friendship love is rooted in a pleasurable glow of the heart, kindled by genuine affection, fondness, and liking.

Sexual love

The Greeks used the word *eros* from which we get our word "erotic." This is passion, exhilarating excitement, on-fire emotions. Eros is not intrinsically evil. Erotic love is a marvelous gift from God, but it can be twisted and perverted.

---

114. Beckwith, *Your Winning Edge*, 217–220.

Sexual love is *passion-based*; biological love is *parent-based*; friendship love is *pleasure-based*; and the next type of love, *agape* love, is *prizing-based*.

Agapē love

This is the highest expression of love, the pinnacle, the summit. The Greeks used the word *agapeo* in describing this type of love. This is the most frequent word for love in the New Testament, appearing over three hundred times in its various forms. This is highly unusual because the Greek poets and philosophers rarely used the word *agapē*. They considered it extremely rare if not humanly impossible. What is agapē love?

Friendship love is based on a pleasurable, reciprocal relationship between two people; agape love is based on prizing or valuing someone. Agapē "speaks of a love which is awakened by a sense of value in an object which causes one to prize it."[115]

Since God intended sexual love exclusively for the marital union of a man and a woman, marriage alone offers love in all four dimensions. In a Spirit-filled marriage, agapē love includes the other three types of love: sexual, biological, and friendship. Biological love is the bond of oneness ("bone of my bones, and flesh of my flesh" Gen. 2:23), friendship love is the pleasure of companionship, sexual love is the intimacy of passion, and agapē love is valuing each other as a priceless treasure. Four-dimensional love is God's ultimate for a human relationship.

God gives us agapē love, even when we're unlovable. He's in the salvaging business. He loves the discarded, the shamed, the bruised, the hurting. When a friendship has long been discarded due to violations in the relationships, agapē reaches out, placing value on the person. This is the love of God. "God is so rich in

115. Kenneth S. Wuest, *Bypaths in the Greek New Testament* (Grand Rapids, MI: Wm. B. Eerdmans Publishing Co., 1940), 109–110.

mercy, and he loved us so much, that even though we were dead because of our sins, he gave us life when he raised Christ from the dead. (It is only by God's grace that you have been saved!)" (Eph. 2:4–5 NLT).

This is the love God had for the people of Nineveh. In his love, he withdrew the judgment they deserved. Now he is confronting Jonah: What's wrong with you, Jonah? Where is your compassion? I loved you enough to rescue you from certain death in the stomach of that fish. Can't you love the Ninevites who have turned from their evil ways? Instead of a pity party for yourself, can't you have pity on these people?

HOW DO I BUILD A LOVING LIFE?

Since it isn't eternally important how many awards and plaques I receive, how many possessions I have, how many degrees I've earned, how many things I've achieved, how much applause I receive, how do I live for what counts. How do I build a loving life?

There are many misconceptions of love. Is love just being nice all the time? Do I allow others to trample me? Is love refusing to stand up to someone? No.

BUILDING BLOCKS FOR LOVE

Love is not just a syrupy, gushy sentiment. It is not just feelings and emotions. We think of love as something that happens on some enchanted evening across a crowded room. Is the love still there on some exhausted evening when the two-year-old is sick for the third time this month, you've been laid off from your job, the electricity is about to be turned off, the washing machine quit, and the stack of unpaid bills seems higher than your wedding cake? It will take more than euphoric feelings from some enchanted evening to make it through some exhausted evening.[116]

Since love is what matters most, how do I build a life of love? Start by applying the three A's below in all your relationships.

ACCEPT ONE ANOTHER

> Therefore, accept one another, just as Christ also accepted us to the glory of God. (Rom. 15:7)

What does this mean? "Accept" means to "receive" rather than "reject." We're prone to confuse accept with acceptable. It doesn't mean, "I accept you once you straighten up, I accept you when you stop doing ..." It means to receive without reservation. It means I love you ... no matter what. Unconditional love removes the *ifs*. It is not love when you say, "I love you *if* you don't disappoint me. I love you *if* you change your behavior. I love you *if* you don't hurt me. I love you *if* I continue to have feelings for you."

Accepting another person is not condoning sin or giving them the silent treatment—an unspoken critical attitude. It's a choice, not a feeling. It is placing a high value on the person and seeing the positive potential in a glaring flaw. Love is accepting the total person—strengths and weaknesses. Accepting rather than rejecting is the foundation for them to grow and change.

Accepting someone doesn't give them the right to walk on you. It doesn't accept sin as inconsequential. If your business partner is stealing funds from your company, if your adult child is doing drugs and stealing money, if someone is spreading lies about you, love confronts the wrong. "I am sad that you have made wrong choices. You will have to pay the consequences for

---

116. Beckwith, *Your Winning Edge*, 217–218.

your behavior. However, I don't reject you as a person. My love for you remains constant."

ACKNOWLEDGE WRONGS AND FORGIVE

> When you offer your gift to God at the altar, and you remember that your brother or sister has something against you, leave your gift there at the altar. Go and make peace with that person, and then come and offer your gift. (Matt. 5:23-24 NCV)

> Be kind to one another, tender-hearted, forgiving each other, just as God in Christ also has forgiven you. (Eph. 4:32)

Forgiving and being forgiven are at the core of genuine Christianity. I am surprised by how many Christians will neglect asking forgiveness when they have wronged someone or refuse to forgive others.

I can understand when someone says, "I am struggling to forgive that person." This is quite different than saying, "I am unwilling to forgive that person." Unwillingness to forgive is a huge problem. It is non-Christian. I always ask the unforgiving person, "Do you want the Lord to forgive you?" Of course, they do. The words of Jesus are clear. "If you forgive those who sin against you, your heavenly Father will forgive you. But if you refuse to forgive others, your Father will not forgive your sins" (Matt. 6:14–15 NLT).

Not only are we commanded to forgive, but Jesus also instructed us to do good and pray for those who have wronged us. "Love your enemies, do good to those who hate you, bless those who curse you, pray for those who mistreat you" (Luke 6:27–28).

APPRECIATE AND ENCOURAGE DAILY

> Encourage one another and build up one another, just as you also are doing. (1 Thess. 5:11)

> Encourage one another day after day, as long as it is still called "Today," so that none of you will be hardened by the deceitfulness of sin. (Heb. 3:13)

Encouraging others is not optional. It's a command. Encouraging others is not something to be done occasionally—once or twice a year—but daily. Encouraging others is essential. Failure to encourage contributes to a hardness of heart and increased vulnerability to temptation.

Some believers I know well just don't do encouraging. "Not my thing," they say. I don't think they would give a word of encouragement to save the life of their grandmother. On the flip side, I often find they are starved for encouragement, so they find it difficult to encourage someone else. But do you say to your fireplace, "Give me some warmth, and I'll give you some wood"? Initiate encouraging others and plenty of warmth will come your way.

Encourage someone today. Congratulate a co-worker on work well done, appreciate a friend's smile, compliment a neighbor for her consistent character, thank your spouse for being there, and do it with honesty. It's like oxygen for a person's soul. You can't build a life of love without being an encourager of others.

APPRECIATE AND **E**NCOURAGE **D**AILY

"God values you so much and I do too. I want to encourage and build you up every day."

ACKNOWLEDGE **W**RONGS AND **F**ORGIVE

"I will own it when I'm wrong and ask forgiveness when I hurt you. Christ has forgiven me, and you can count on my full forgiveness of you."

ACCEPT **O**NE **A**NOTHER

"I accept you as a person—strengths and weaknesses. I won't play God in your life and attempt to change you. I trust God's work in your life ... in his time and in his way."

CHOOSING TO LOVE ...

LOVE CHANGES THINGS

Living a life of love will change your life—all for good.

LOVE WILL ...

... change how you treat your employees.

... change how you treat your boss.

... prevent you from being an obnoxious, irritating, self-centered, rude person.

... transform your attitude toward life.

... affect how you drive your car.

... bring your anger under control.

... transform how you treat your friends.

... transform how you treat your former friends (enemies).

... persevere through the toughest of times.

... mystify your neighbor.

... soften the soil of a hardened heart.

200

... set you free from resentment.

... change how you treat your spouse.

... set you free from self-pity.

... keep you from stewing over someone's success.

... change what you post on Facebook and the internet.

... change how you treat the outcast, destitute, and lonely.

... change how you treat those with different skin color.

... change how you treat those in the other political party.[117]

---

117. Some of the points attributed to an unknown source.

LOVE YOUR NEIGHBOR

A self-justifying lawyer asked Jesus what he needed to do to inherit eternal life. As Jesus often did, he responded to a question with a question. "What is written in the Law? How does it read to you?" (Luke 10:26). The lawyer was well-schooled and gave a superb answer. "YOU SHALL LOVE THE LORD YOUR GOD WITH ALL YOUR HEART, AND WITH ALL YOUR SOUL, AND WITH ALL YOUR STRENGTH, AND WITH ALL MIND; AND YOUR NEIGHBOR AS YOURSELF" (v. 27). Jesus replied, "You have answered correctly; DO THIS AND YOU WILL LIVE." (v. 28). The lawyer, wishing to justify himself, replied, "And who is my neighbor?" (v. 29).

This was a loaded question, ripe for quibbling. According to the scribes and Pharisees, neighbors were your Jewish friends who adhered to the law. They did not consider tax collectors, prostitutes, Gentiles, and most of all, Samaritans to be neighbors. They were on their "people we can't stand" list. Consequently, they felt justified in despising and hating them. Jonah's feelings toward the Ninevites fit with this line of thinking. He probably muttered to himself, *I love the world (all my Jewish friends) … it's people (like Ninevites) I can't stand.*

While the lawyer wanted to wrangle, Jesus answered his question with a zinger of a story that must have left him with his jaw dangling.

> Jesus replied and said, "A man was going down from Jerusalem to Jericho, and fell among robbers, and they stripped him and beat him, and went away leaving himhalf dead. And by chance a priest was going down on that road, and when he saw him, he passed by on the other side. Likewise, a Levite also, when he came to the place and saw him, passed by on the other side. But a Samaritan, who was on a journey, came upon him; and when he saw him, he felt compassion, and came to him and bandaged up his wounds, pouring

oil and wine on them; and he put him on his own beast, and brought him to an inn and took care of him. On the next day he took out two denarii and gave them to the innkeeper and said, 'Take care of him; and whatever more you spend, when I return, I will repay you.' Which of these three do you think proved to be a neighbor to the man who fell into the robbers' hands?" And he said, "The one who showed mercy toward him." Then Jesus said to him, "Go and do the same." (Luke 10:30–37)

Who is my neighbor? The word "neighbor" is a compound word from "neigh" meaning someone who is "near" and "bor" from the Anglo-Saxon word *bur, gebur,* or *boor*—meaning a farmer or property owner of the lowest class, peasant, countryman, or a boor (a person who is an unmannerly person, rustic, yokel, a country bumpkin).[118] *Merriam-Webster* defines *boor* as a peasant or a rude, insensitive person.[119] Really? A rude or insensitive person? A country bumpkin?

I ask myself: *What does this mean for who is MY neighbor?* Here's how I unpack it. "My neighbor" is someone near or within my sphere of influence—in my neighborhood, a fellow employee, a clerk in the store, an obnoxious person I meet on my walk, an atheist or Muslim who comes to live with us, a Hispanic laborer, an irritating relative, or someone living in the inner city or under a bridge. My neighbor may be within my sphere of influence by email or text. My neighbor may be overseas if I can do something to help them. But most of all, I can't say, "I love all the people in Africa while showing no concern for the person living near me."

118. *Dictionary.com*, s.v. "neighbor," "boor. accessed Mar. 31, 2019, https://www.dictionary.com/browse/neighbor and https://www.dictionary.com/browse/boor.

119. *Merriam-Webster Dictionary*, s.v. "boor," accessed Mar. 31, 2019, https://www.merriam-webster.com/dictionary/boor

"My neighbor" certainly includes but is not limited to the people I care for and enjoy hanging out with like my Bible study group, my bike riding buddies, my pastoral friends, my church family, and members of my family. However, my neighbor goes beyond the "I like" group of people in my life—and it *must* go beyond. Neighbors include those with different colors of skin, religious beliefs, economic status, or political party. Being a neighbor doesn't require that I agree with them. In other words, my neighbors include people "I like" … and people "I can't stand."

I try to begin my day like Mr. Rogers, "Won't you be my neighbor?" I smile, seek to be friendly, value them, look for those in need … though I rarely wear a sweater. It's my goal to slow down enough to give a kind word or listen to someone in need.

It is possible to take this in a legalistic way—to feel guilt-ridden over every needy person and every urgent cause that comes my way. I can't meet all the needs that come across my path nor do I believe God wants me to. Instead, God wants me to be *willing* to care for whoever he brings across my path, willing to help when it is within my power to do so. I need to be sensitive to the leading of the Spirit in my life. I am not under bondage to meet every need—I am choosing to live a life of love, spreading God's love wherever I can.

HOW TO BE A LOVING NEIGHBOR

Looking back at the story Jesus told, the Samaritan showed us what it means to be a loving neighbor. Here is how to be a person filled with compassion using your eyes, ears, heart, and hands.

First, begin by *seeing* the needs of people around you. "When he saw him …" (Luke 10:3). Look around you. Study people.

Read their faces. What do their facial expressions convey? Is this person disturbed or anxious? Develop spiritual radar.

Second, *listen* for the emotional needs of others. "He felt compassion, ..." (v. 33). By observing and listening, he developed a heart of compassion. Ask God to give you ears that hear and a heart of compassion.

Third, use your *hands* to care. The Samaritan "came to him and bandaged up his wounds, pouring oil and wine on them; and he put him on his own beast, and brought him to an inn and took care of him" (Luke 10:33). Love became action. He did what he was capable of doing. He didn't agree to pay all his future debts—just enough to cover his recovery.

"Go and do the same" (v. 37) is Jesus speaking to you and me.

It isn't every day we'll see someone lying by the road, robbed, and beaten. We're more likely to meet our neighbors as we chat outside our garage or lend them a cup of flour. They have needs though they are not as visible. To open the door for deeper caring and sharing the gospel, here are some ideas to plant seeds with your neighbors.

IDEAS TO PREPARE THE NEIGHBORHOOD FOR THE GOSPEL

◊ Bake bread, cookies, or a pie and take it to neighbors.

◊ Host a block party or a Christmas gathering.

◊ Offer childcare for a couple with young children or a single parent.

◊ Offer to paint the curb numbers for your neighbors.

◊ Take dinner over on the day a new family moves in.

◊ Offer to clean the rain gutters for your neighbors.

◊ Host a move-in welcoming party.

◊ Hold a bike fix-up clinic.

◊ Invite the neighbors for a shared soup and salad evening.

◊ Assist the elderly or single moms with household repairs.

◊ Offer to mow a neighbor's lawn.

◊ Take some fresh-cut flowers to a neighbor.

◊ Celebrate your neighbor's birthday or anniversary.

◊ Develop a neighborhood volleyball or softball team.

◊ Host a Neighborhood Watch evening to discuss home security issues (invite a police officer to address preventative measures).

◊ Offer to wash your neighbor's car or host a neighborhood car wash party.

◊ Buy extra strawberries and share some with the neighbors.

◊ Give a copy of the movie seen by more people in all of history, *Jesus*.

◊ Develop a neighborhood walking or biking club.

JONAH CHAPTER FIVE

Before you look for this in your Bible, there is no chapter five in Jonah. Just my wishful thinking. We really don't know the rest of the story. I would like to think that Jonah returned to Nineveh and loved the people. Wouldn't it be great if Jonah chapter five went something like this?

JONAH 5

¹ The word of the LORD came to Jonah a third time. "Go the great city. Live among them. Teach them my ways."

² Jonah bristled as he heard the words, but before saying no he thought about the last time he said no. "Not too bright," he thought to himself.

³ Looking down the hillside, he saw a group of people kneeling in prayer. The heart of Jonah was pierced. Returning to his shelter, he sat down and wept bitterly. "Oh, great and awesome God, how could I be so selfish and stubborn. I ask that you forgive me for my hardness of heart. I need to repent just like the people in that great city."

⁴ Jonah slept very little that night. He could hear the rejoicing in the city below, and he continued to think about what God had told him to do.

⁵ When morning arrived, Jonah made his way into the city. Was this the same place? He walked past idols that had been smashed. He saw a shop where astrological forecasts had been made for years. No more lines of people wondering and worrying about their future. The sign on the shop said "Closed."

⁶ The farther he walked, the more amazed he became. No one was staggering down the street intoxicated. Children were playing in the streets without fear. No one was swearing or beating their animals. However, some of the animals were confused when they received orders that weren't barked with profanity. Former prostitutes were now collecting food to give to the poor. Families were being reunited.

⁷ Jonah wept as he walked through the city—broken that he had hated these people so fiercely.

⁸ Recognized as the prophet who pronounced doom on the city, they gathered around Jonah. "Great is the LORD. He has forgiven us!" they shouted.

⁹ Feeling awkward because his prophecy hadn't come to pass, Jonah finally asked, "What are your needs now? What can I do to help?" They explained that a large remnant of people living by the river lacked food and shelter. When the king asked Jonah to meet with him, Jonah explained the need. The king said, "Let's organize the people to provide homes and food for these people."

¹⁰ In the years that followed Jonah taught the people the ways of God while he initiated the hugely popular Ninevite Bible Clubs for the kids. Often, he would go by the river and help people do their laundry. They smiled with gratitude.

¹¹ The people loved this prophet who brought them the message of warning, and Jonah, in turn, loved them. Though he was a Jew, he saw a different side to the Assyrian people—even though they were the dreaded enemies of Israel.

¹² When Jonah was nearing death, several of his closest Ninevite friends surrounded his bedside, caring for his every need. After his long ministry in Nineveh, Jonah was buried in the center of the city with great honors.

I may be way off base. Perhaps Jonah continued in his self-centered, bigoted way. I hope not. Two things give me a glimmer of hope.

First, a traditional burial site for Jonah is in Nineveh.

Why would he be buried there if he did not live there and love the people of Nineveh?

Second, I believe Jonah told his own story.

Who else would have known the details of the storm and his experience inside the fish? Who else would have known the details of his anger and depression? While the book is written mostly in the third person, it bears the mark of a personal memoir. Most scholars believe Jonah penned his own story. If Jonah had remained in his angry, depressed, and bigoted state of mind, would the Holy Spirit have used him to write scripture?

I look forward to seeing Jonah in heaven and hearing the rest of the story!

THE JONAH JOURNEY OF BROKENNESS CONTINUES

It is not uncommon for young pastors, fresh out of seminary with heads full of information, to preach *at* the people. That was me. "Straighten up, read your Bible every day, start serving, show up for Sunday morning and evening and Wednesday night prayer meeting, get committed, give 'til it hurts … do, do, do, do!" All good things.

But then God leads his servant through a series of heart-wrenching experiences—a violent storm in relationships, an overboard experience of wanting to quit the ministry, drowning in expectations he can't meet, simmering anger, burn out and depression. God is breaking the vessel, preparing a message of sweetness to spill out. A new pastor emerges—a different person who still has blue eyes and a quirky laugh. But he laughs more now. Messages have the same truth but a different tone—they are filled with compassion and understanding. Grace-driven instead of guilt-driven. Numbers aren't nearly as important. Love is the goal.

WHAT'S THE NEXT CHAPTER IN YOUR LIFE?

Yesterdays are gone. God is leading you through your own journey of brokenness. Believe me, it is not without purpose. With every twist and turn, every failure and disappointment, every scar and wound, your heavenly Father is watching over you and has your best interests at heart. He is faithfully shaping you, softening your heart, teaching you to grieve for others, and yearning to demonstrate his love through your life for all your remaining days. Brokenness is the key that opens the door of blessing.

God designed you—not to have pitiful pity parties—but to be filled and overflowing with his presence. Abraham Lincoln said, "To ease another's heartache is to forget one's own."

Wake up and stay up.

Look for the lonely. Be a friend.

Care for the brokenhearted.

Encourage someone every day.

Let church squabbles be gone.

Forgive as you've been forgiven.

Let's "LOVE THE WORLD—*AND* THE PEOPLE WE CAN'T STAND!"

One thing is crystal clear from the book of Jonah: GOD LOVES THE LOST!

WHICH IS IT?
"… may the saved get lost!" or "… may the lost get saved!"

TIME OUT

CHAPTER SEVEN

WHAT MATTERS MOST

If I could speak in any language in heaven or on earth but didn't love others, I would only be making meaningless noise like a loud gong or a clanging cymbal. (1 Cor. 13:1 NLT)

GROW AND APPLY

◊ Read Jonah 4:5–11 and 1 Cor. 13:1–8.

◊ Who is the most loving person you've ever known?

_____

_____

_____

_____

_____

_____

◊ What were the characteristics that made them this way?

_____

_____

_____

_____

_____

_____

PRAY

During your time of prayer, go through these fifteen attributes of love from 1 Corinthians 13. Ask God to apply them in your relationship with someone you've had a hard time loving. Make some notes of things you need to do to build a life of love.

1. *Love is patient* with the faults of others—accepting them and trusting God to bring about change in his time.

2. *Love is kind*—gracious, thoughtful, and sensitive to build up rather than tear down.

3. *Love is not envious*—undercutting, spiteful, jealous.

4. *Love is not boastful*—self-centered, pushy to get its own way.

5. *Love is not proud*—not displaying an independent, stubborn spirit, resisting advice, refusing to acknowledge wrongs and ask forgiveness.

6. *Love is not rude*—not insensitive, irritable, touchy, making a scene.

7. *Love is not self-seeking*—instead, it is flexible, gentle, easy to work with, not demanding its own way.

8. *Love is not easily angered*—popping off, easily provoked, hot-headed.

9. *Love keeps no record of wrongs*—doesn't hold a grudge or bring up the past but chooses to forgive.

10. *Love does not delight in evil*—divisive, spreading gossip, taking revenge, practicing deceit— *but rejoices with the truth.*

11. *Love always protects* the reputation of others—seeking to give a good report, remaining loyal, and guarding confidential information.

12. *Love always trusts*—believing what God can do.

13. *Love always hopes*—anticipating what God will do.

14. *Love always perseveres*—enduring despite hardships and misunderstandings.

15. *Love never fails*—never giving up or falling away.

SHARE

Look for opportunities to share your faith. Here are a couple of thought-provoking questions to ask when the time is right.

1. What matters most in life for you?
2. Why isn't there more love in our world?

TIME TOGETHER

CHAPTER SEVEN

WHAT MATTERS MOST

If you're leading a small group, teaching a Bible class, or sharing with the family, below are some opening questions. For the content of the lesson, use the Grow and Apply, Prayer, and Share sections with your Time Out.

CONNECT
(choose one or two for discussion)

◊ True or false? Love makes the world go 'round.

◊ True or false? Love makes the arms go 'round.

◊ With knowledge exploding, why do we still have wars, crime, terrorism, cheating, and racism? Is more knowledge the answer?

APPENDIX A

THREE SIMPLE STEPS TO NEW LIFE

Beginning the Christian life is as simple as the ABCs backward. Today you can begin the most thrilling adventure of your life as a follower of Jesus Christ. Here's how.

Confess your sins. You may have lived a good, moral life, but the Bible says, "All have sinned and fall short of the glory of God" (Rom. 3:23), and "the wages of sin is death, but the gift of God is eternal life in Christ Jesus our Lord" (Rom. 6:23). The Bible also says, "God showed his great love for us by sending Christ to die for us while we were still sinners" (Rom. 5:8 NLT). Jesus Christ shed his blood on the cross to pay the penalty for your sins and to provide complete forgiveness. Confess your sins and ask Christ to forgive your sins. God "… is patient toward you, not wishing for any to perish but for all to come to repentance" (2 Pet. 3:9).

Believe in Jesus Christ as your Savior and Lord. When a religious man asked Jesus how to get to heaven, Jesus told him, "For God loved the world so much that he gave his one and only Son, so that everyone who believes in him will not perish but have eternal life" (John 3:16 NLT). Believing in Jesus Christ is a simple choice and a step of faith. "If you confess with your mouth that Jesus is Lord and believe in your heart that God raised him from the dead, you will be saved" (Rom. 10:9 NLT).

Accept **Christ into your life.** The Bible says, "To all who believed him and accepted him, he gave the right to become children of God. They are reborn—not with a physical birth resulting from human passion or plan, but a birth that comes from God" (John 1:12–13 NLT). By accepting or asking Christ into your life, he now lives within you. "This is the secret: Christ lives in you" (Col. 1:27 NLT).

Dear God,
I confess my sin. Thank you that you forgive every sin because of Christ's death on the cross.
I believe in Jesus Christ. I place my faith and trust in him. He proved himself to be God through his miraculous life, his death on the cross, and resurrection from the dead.
I accept Jesus Christ into my life. By your Spirit, I invite you to live within me.

Signed: _____

Date:_____

APPENDIX B

A GUIDE FOR SMALL GROUPS

The shared journey is the best journey. If you went on a cruise to Alaska or snorkeling in the Caribbean, would you rather go alone or have a friend to share the experience with? When you see something beautiful or experience something spectacular, you naturally want to tell someone about it. God designed us with a need to connect, to share our joys as well as our sorrows with someone who understands. The impact of your six-week personal growth journey will be doubled when others travel with you. Select one or two other people to share the journey with or develop a small group with several participants. Don't miss the joy of the shared journey.

WHY SMALL GROUPS?

In this world driven to achieve big results and big crowds, small groups may seem ... well, small ... as in insignificant and unimportant. God disagrees. The ancient prophet asked, "Who has despised the day of small things?" (Zech. 4:10). Small groups are God's idea for fellowship. You can worship with a large crowd, but you can't fellowship with five thousand people. The big crowd fosters loneliness; the small group builds friendships.

ARE SMALL GROUPS BIBLICAL?

From the earliest days of the Church, the believers met in small groups, usually in someone's home. After the conversion and baptism of 3,000 (recorded in Acts 2:38–41), they began meeting together for teaching, fellowship, prayer, and breaking of bread from house to house (Acts 2:42, 46). This was authentic Christianity at the cell level. As the Church continued to grow and persecution broke out, Acts 5:42 says, "Every day, in the temple and from house to house, they kept right on teaching and preaching Jesus as the Christ" (Acts 5:42). Before Paul became a follower of Jesus, he was ravaging the church, going house to house as they met and dragging Christians off to prison (Acts 8:3). After God got hold of his life and spun him around, Paul went from terrorizing believers house to house to teaching believers house to house (Acts 20:20). Paul also mentions a church in the house of Aquila and Priscilla (Rom. 16:3, 5; 1 Cor. 16:19), Gaius (Rom. 16:23), Philemon (Philem. 1, 2), and Nympha in Laodicea (Col. 4:15).

The intimacy of the home and the dynamic of the small group provide a natural setting for spiritual growth, but groups can meet wherever it works—a coffee shop, restaurant, at the workplace, or in a park. You name the setting, and Jesus will meet you there. A small group can be two or three people or as many as twelve to fifteen. And remember, the Lord is present whenever you meet. The presence of Jesus makes your group, large or small, an exciting place to be.

TIPS FOR LEADING A SMALL GROUP

Being a facilitator for a small group is not as difficult as it may seem. You don't have to be a preacher or even a great talker. If you're taking the lead in a small group, here are some tips.

1. **Prepare in advance.** Read the Bible passages, think through the questions, and pray for the members of the group before each session.

2. **Don't do it all yourself.** Before you begin, if possible, select a co-leader to assist you and to lead from time to time. Have someone else coordinate a refreshment schedule so everyone brings something. You may also want to rotate homes.

3. **Introduce newcomers.** Make certain everyone knows the others in the group by name. The Connect section that opens each session is designed to facilitate knowing each other personally and deepening your relationships.

4. **Prepare a group roster.** Have a group member make a list of the names, phone numbers, and email addresses of group members and

distribute a copy to each person. Don't forget to update it when a new person joins the group.

5. **Relax and be who you are.** Rather than worrying about the impression you're making on others, greet each person with a warm smile. Be interested in them and enjoy laughing together. If someone asks a question you don't have an answer to, say so. You don't have to be a know-it-all. They will respect you for being a learner with them.

6. **Ask questions and listen.** Being an effective group leader is more about listening than telling. The questions included with each session are designed for discussion. If you add questions of your own, don't use closed-ended questions. These are questions that are answered with a yes or no or require no more than a one- or two-word answer. They close off a discussion. Instead, use open-ended questions. For example, instead of asking "Do you think this is important?" ask "Why do you think this is important?" Ask "How did you feel when …?" or "What would you recommend to someone facing this situation?" Don't panic if you ask a question, and there isn't an immediate response. Be patient as group members gather their thoughts.

7. **Rotate around the group for Scripture reading.** To involve everyone, have each person read one or two verses.

8. **Affirm the responses of group members.** After someone shares, show your appreciation by saying something like, "Thanks for sharing that" or "That was a helpful insight." Then for those who haven't shared, ask, "Would someone else like to add to this?" or "We haven't had the opportunity to hear from everyone on this. Who else would like to share?" Even if someone gives a wrong answer, don't put them down. Gently give another perspective. Be sensitive to those who are new or reluctant to speak up or pray out loud. Give them a safe place. As they begin to feel more comfortable, they'll come along. Don't force or pressure them.

9. **Don't allow one or two people to dominate the discussion.** If an individual is taking over the discussion, say something like, "Thank you, Joe, for sharing. And since we haven't heard from the others, let's hear what they have to offer." If it continues to be a problem, meet alone with him, where you can say something like, "Joe, I'm pleased you're part of the group, and you have good things to share. However, I want to ask you to help me help the quieter members participate equally. Please give a brief comment, and then let's pass the opportunity to others."

10. **Break into smaller groups.** If your group is larger than seven people, divide into smaller groups of two to four people for part of the session. This is also an effective setting for prayer. The quieter person will feel more comfortable praying out loud when the group is smaller. This smaller group can become a "prayer partnership." Encourage them to be in touch during the week by phone, email, or text.

11. **Pray and worship together.** Allow individuals to share their prayer concerns and then take the time to pray for each other. Encourage short prayers. Occasionally you may want the group to pray using one-sentence prayers. This can be particularly effective when praising God for his attributes and blessings. Sometimes you'll want to stand and join hands in a circle as you pray. This creates a strong sense of unity. Music can also be a vital part of prayer. If someone plays an instrument, you can ask them to lead in a simple song of praise. Or you can select a song on a Christian CD and play it as the group sings along. Make certain the song is not too difficult for singing as a group.

12. **Go with the flow.** It isn't necessary to cover all the questions. Be flexible. Make certain the meeting doesn't go too long. A good discussion can continue after the group is dismissed if this is acceptable to the host.

TIPS FOR HOSTING A SMALL GROUP

The thought of others coming to your home can be quite intimidating. If you're uptight about making a good impression, you will have difficulty enjoying the group. Instead of feeling you have to entertain your guests, choose to relax and give hospitality to your guests. Here are the crucial differences.

ENTERTAINING VERSUS SHOWING HOSPITALITY

There is a world of difference between entertaining and hospitality. Entertaining seeks to impress others; hospitality seeks to be interested in others. When you're entertaining, you're constantly asking yourself, "What are they thinking? Am I making a good impression?" With hospitality, the focus is on your guest, not on yourself. Ask caring questions. Listen with love and understanding. Often, entertaining creates pressure to perform, which then creates fear and nervousness. Hospitality is different. You can tell when you're practicing hospitality because it will almost always be a joyful experience. You sense God using you to show love to others. Peter reminded the believers, "Most important of all, continue to show deep love for each other, for love covers a multitude of sins. Cheerfully share your home with those who need a meal or a place to stay" (1 Pet. 4:8–9 NLT).

What is important for your guests?

Think through the last time you were invited as a guest to someone's home. Check below what was *essential* for you to feel comfortable and welcomed. This will help you know what is really important when people come to your home.

◊ Home spotlessly clean and closets organized
◊ Silver tea service, imported cups, and saucers
◊ Feeling the host was glad you came
◊ Windows washed, and carpets cleaned
◊ Furnishings that could be featured in *Home & Decor*
◊ The host asks how your week has been
◊ Home comfortably clean
◊ Fresh-cut flowers
◊ Gourmet entrees and expensive desserts
◊ Relaxed setting
◊ Feeling accepted as a person
◊ Healthy and tasty snacks
◊ Kick-your-shoes-off comfortable
◊ Being listened to

SMALL GROUP GUIDELINES

To keep things on track, ask the group to commit to some practices that make for a healthy group. At the beginning of a new study, read through these guidelines, discuss, and agree to practice them. This may be duplicated for the group.

1. **Focused and Balanced**. We meet to worship God, fellowship together, grow in the Word of God, apply the Word to our lives to serve others, and share our faith with unbelievers.

2. **Group Attendance**. To stay in touch with one another, we will call, text, or send an email if we are unable to attend or running late. This will be our goal for when the group starts and ends: Arrival time: _____ Starting time: _____ Ending time: _____These are the calendar dates we will be meeting: _____ _____

3. **Guard Confidences**. We will be careful to avoid sharing confidential information outside the group.

4. **Healthy Group Life**. We will be careful to avoid dominating the conversation, and we will always look for the opportunity for everyone to share. We will seek to make this a safe place where others can share their struggles without receiving a snap judgment or a quick fix to their problem. We will be sensitive to the special

needs of group members. Some may have to leave for work at 4:30 a.m., so we will be careful not to go too late; some may have dietary restrictions so we will be alert to these when planning refreshments or a meal together; and some may be struggling with alcohol, so we recognize it is best not to serve alcoholic beverages.

5. **Welcome Newcomers**. We will look for opportunities to invite friends and warmly welcome newcomers to the group.

ABOUT THE AUTHOR

Dave Beckwith grew up in the Midwest in a small town of seven hundred fifty people, Murdo, South Dakota (and some other small towns). In first grade when the teacher asked what everyone wanted to be … fireman, teacher, doctor, nurse, etc., Dave announced he was going to be a pastor. The call of God on his life was clear from this early age, shortly after he committed his life to Christ. During high school, he preached his first sermons in the small church.

In the fall of 1965, Dave started Biola where he met his future wife, Joanne. She recorded meal ticket numbers in the cafeteria—Dave's number was 573, and she had his number. One week after their wedding in 1969, Dave and Joanne began their journey in pastoral ministry. And what an adventure it has been—some thrilling joys and successes along with struggles, pain, and setbacks. God has repeatedly spared Dave's life ... a knife thrown at him while preaching in the Philippines, a dramatic rescue from a fiery head-on freeway collision with a drunk driver who was driving on the wrong side of the freeway, a forty-foot fall while speaking in Northern California, and a biking accident when the driver of an SUV plowed into and ran over him. Dave relates these life lessons and many others in his speaking and teaching.

Dave's ministry experience includes youth and camp ministry, church administration, and serving as a senior pastor for over thirty years. Currently, Dave and Joanne serve as shepherds with Standing Stone Ministry, caring for spiritual leaders. Dave is also the Western US Regional Director for Standing Stone Ministry, training and coordinating the work of over fifty pastoral shepherds. In 2007, Dave was named senior pastor emeritus for Woodbridge Church in Irvine, California, where he served as senior pastor for nearly twenty years.

Dave and Joanne also wrote *Your Winning Edge: God's Power Perfected in Weakness* (previously titled *The Edge*). The third edition will soon be released by Elk Lake Publishing, Inc. Dave and Joanne are both graduates of Biola University. Joanne received her BS degree in nursing. Professionally, she has worked in alcohol and drug rehab and psychiatry. Dave received his BS degree in business administration at Biola and did his seminary work at Talbot School of Theology. Additional graduate studies have included an MA in biblical studies and a PhD in church and family ministry.

A love for God's beauty in nature takes them on hikes and rides on their recumbent bikes. Their two married daughters, Julie and Tami, four grandchildren, and seven great-grandchildren are a great source of joy and enjoyment.

Having faced the painful side of personal and church life has equipped them to come alongside others. God has given them a heart for those who hurt and a shared life mission to help others discover God's power in their weakest moments. One of their greatest joys is sharing over a cup of coffee or a meal—weeping with those who weep and rejoicing with those who rejoice.

You may contact Dave for speaking, consulting, or leader care at:

Standing Stone Ministry
270 Baker Street East, Suite 100, Costa Mesa, CA 92626
dave.b@standingstoneministry.org
www.standingstoneministry.org or www.pastorbiker.com

Made in the USA
San Bernardino, CA
03 September 2019